AF255365

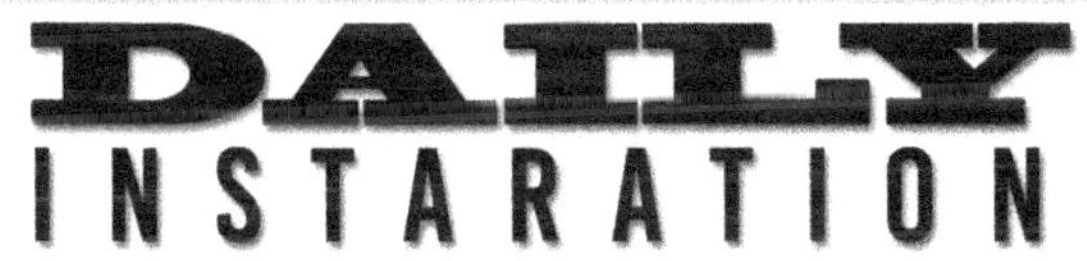

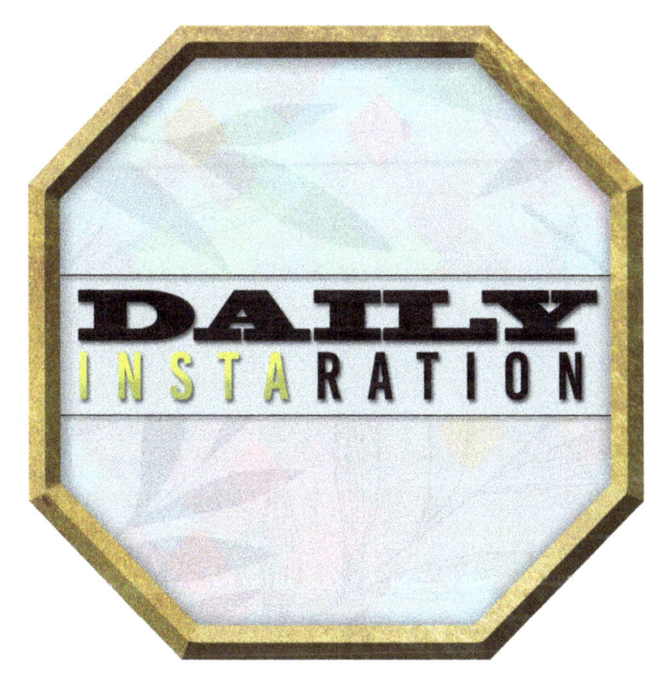

AMANDA SCHAEFER

ILLUSTRATED BY
JACKSON SCHAEFER

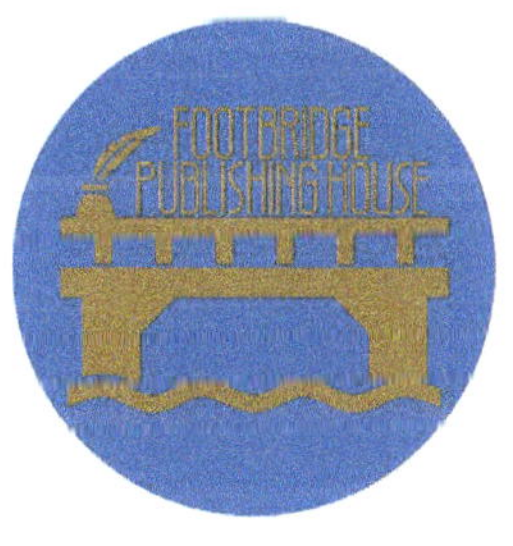

ISBN: 978-0-578-64470-7 (Paperback)

Printed by Ingram Spark, in the United States of America.
First Printing 2020.

Cover, illustrations, and book design
by Jackson Schaefer

Pattern of leaves used on front cover designed by pikisuperstar / Freepik

For information contact
Footbridge Publishing House

www.footbridgepublishinghouse.com

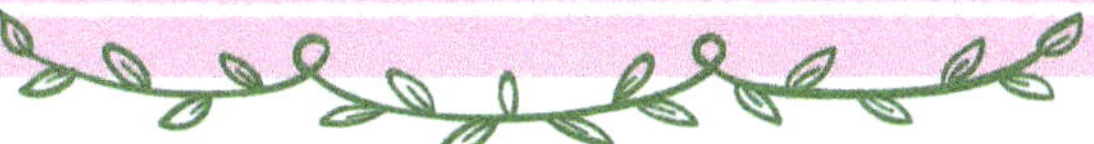

This book is dedicated to my amazing
family who ceaselessly supports me with
nonstop encouragement and love.

I am so grateful for you all!

Foreword

I asked people from the online community this book explores to share their thoughts with me in order to be part of a collective foreword for this book. I am humbled and excited to share their words as they prove without a doubt that this experiment was a success.

"You remind me of all the ways God is working. How He shows up in the ordinary to minister truth, encouragement, and love to us."

"I have been profoundly affected by your posts. Your positivity, energy, and heartfelt wisdom encourages me to listen to the Angels of my better nature. My heart smiles every time I see your content."

"I love following you, Amanda. Gentle reminders of our Savior in a world of distractions. You point to the Father! And give all the glory to God!"

"Not sure how to word it: listening to or reading your posts I am either over here smiling with a long yes on my heart as you spoke something I either feel, have encountered or that encourages me and sometimes you also clarify, or help me understand deeper as you are more mature in you walk with Jesus and your encounters help me grow!"

"Where to begin. You have impacted my life with your posts in so many ways. Your encouragement and inspiration - the way you find God in even the smallest things is so amazing! You've made me look at things from perspectives I may not have seen without you! You're such an uplifting person that even if I'm feeling discouraged one day, your posts always lift me up, help me see things in a different way than I wasn't seeing! We may not have met in person love, but I truly feel in my heart you are a kindred spirit! I thank God for bringing you into my life! God bless you!"

"Your words often speak directly to me — a shared experience (we haven't met) or an encouragement that I need. Also, I feel people probably think I am crazy if I share my 'little' blessings (like seeing a deer or hearing a song in the wind), but you share such great 'little' blessings that warm my heart and others, and they encourage me to keep looking for those things in my life...And I bought your book 'Crumbled' and enjoyed the longer, thought-provoking ramblings. God bless!"

"Inspired, makes me think, grateful."

"I love your positivity, encouragement, and everyday reminders of how God is there for us in everything! Your posts show your true love for God and your mission to work toward helping His kingdom grow! God bless you!"

Introduction

Content from this book was taken directly from the pages of my Instagram feed. The account was intended to inspire others. The title came simply from bringing the two thoughts together and the name'"Daily Instaration" was born.

When I set up my author account, I wasn't really sure what to expect. I already had a personal account there and was keenly aware of all that social media platforms can bring. I had written a new book and needed to advertise it, but I wanted to try to build a real community. At the very heart of it, what I truly wanted was a group of people I could connect with honestly.

On social media, I have found that many pretend to be someone that they are not. Some individuals strive so much to look like something they want to be that their best qualities tend to take a back seat to their agendas.

If you are on any social media platform, you know the pitfalls of virtual reality. With no direct repercussions for online actions, it is only the individual's sense of what is right that drives their actions. People are using professional equipment to film themselves and others using filters to enhance their natural looks. All of it is so awfully accurate at describing the present state of the world we live in.

I set out to be who I am. I started my account from zero followers instead of changing the name of my existing account and hijacking everyone into following something new without asking for any input from them. I have been on the other end of that scenario, and I decided not to do that to others.

The account started to grow fairly quickly. Over time a few people even asked me to add some videos to my account, and I did. When I filmed myself, I merely held my phone up and spoke. No special makeup. No special lighting. No perfect backdrop. No filters. Just me talking to my online community the way that I speak with my friends because they had become my friends! I talked with them and prayed for them and listened to their struggles. I cheered for them and celebrated their triumphs! They shared their lives with me, prayed for me and encouraged me. These virtual people were real people. They were my people. We had become our own little village, each one of us bringing what we had to offer and all of us receiving somehow all of the things that we needed. Was this really possible? Was this really happening? Was I able to just be myself and still have a successful platform for my books? Apparently so, the account just kept growing.

Some days I shared my DIY projects. Some days I shared about my rescue dog. Some days I shared someone else's encouraging words. Some days I asked questions. And some days, I shared the encouraging words that God had given to me, the ones that lifted me up in a way far beyond well wishes. I shared the words that had given me real hope believing that these encouragements were meant for more than just me. I felt that they were God's heart for all of us.

I wanted to share all of who I am, knowing that sharing my faith might hinder the growth of the account. This was an experiment in being honest about who I was, so I shared everything. The truth is that I am a Christian. I am a writer, a speaker, a publisher, a rescue dog enthusiast, an observer of what God is doing and someone who shares what I see. The truth is my identity in Christ, it is the foundation of everything that I do, of all that I am. It is from that place that I encounter and process the world. In addition to those things, I am also an encourager. As a result of my faith, I can see the beauty in the battle, the triumph in the tragedy, and experience peace in the problematic. I cannot help but share from that perspective. I cannot help but lean on God in the midst of an often unfair and broken world. It was this encouraging attribute that seemed to attract even those who didn't believe what I believed. I set out to share the encouraging words that I knew in my heart people needed to hear.

I have been a participant in creating a real community with people who inspire me and evidently whom I inspire. All of us have invested beyond merely scrolling by and sharing "likes." Instead, we have found a way to share real feelings. I think it starts with one, even just one person, being brave. That authenticity, that vulnerability sets ablaze a wildfire of bravery! It is much like watching popcorn popping, one kernel at a time. At first, just a few kernels react to the heat. Then it seems the entire lot breaks forth popping, becoming, growing, changing from one hard little seed into a joyful explosion of community.

I have loved being part of this family of friends
that have proven to me that the world is still full
of goodness, that God is most definitely still on
His throne, and that being honest is still okay,
even in a world that rarely shows us behind the
curtain.

I am inspired to continue being myself when
there are so many other things that I could
pretend to be. Some days the temptation to
believe that I am not good enough is clamoring
to get into my heart. Still, the truth of my
identity in God is a strong tower that those
accusations cannot invade.

Inside this book, you will find excerpts from my
daily feed from this online community. I share
forty stories with you. I wanted to take a few of
the ideas I have expressed and share them in a
brand new way.

We have added color and lively illustrations to
accentuate the vibrant little gems of my everyday
life. Precious moments that I want you to
experience too. I hope to make more of these as
I go expressing the ordinary moments of the
beautiful life I have been given to live.

I will continue to share my struggles and my
encouragement. I will continue to talk about
things that may not be popular in the world but
will share because they have given me hope,
peace, and purpose. I pray that you will be
blessed by this project.

The idea for this book came from a thought I
had when reading Ecclesiastes Chapter eleven,
verse six in the Bible. It says, "In the morning
sow your seed, and at evening withhold not your
hand, for you do not know which

will prosper, this or that, or whether both alike will be good." (English Standard Version)

The words made me wonder where else I could be sowing my seed like that? Where in the world other than my family and friends could I share the life-giving kernels that God had entrusted me to scatter?

So open up and turn the pages. Look at the pictures and listen to the words. Welcome in. I am so pleased to know you.

01

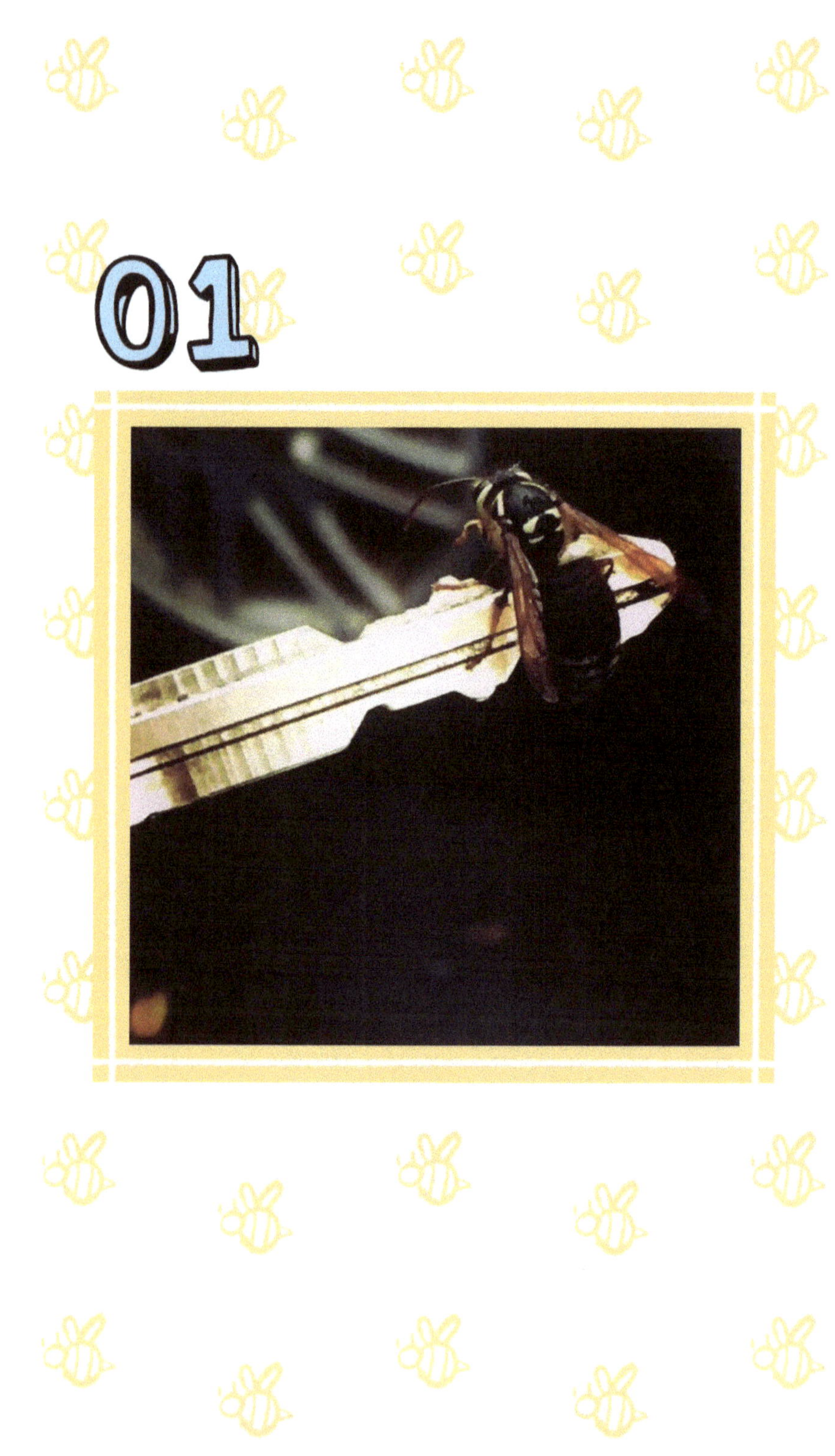

I saw this bee on his back. He was struggling to flip over. He was stuck in the water on the roof of my car. I took my key out and gently flipped him over and he continued to struggle in all of the water on the roof of my car. I tried to pick him up. He tumbled and slid down into the crack of my trunk. I opened the trunk of my car and again took my key and gently helped him out. Eventually, he was able to fly away. Oh, did I mention that I am highly allergic to bees? Yes, I am an "EpiPen" kind of allergic. But here is the thing; I asked God what He was saying to me at this moment. I believe the lesson is this: if you walk by someone and see them struggling, you should stop to try to help them (even if they could hurt you). I knew that I could be wounded, but instead of fearing what could happen to me, I focused on the one who was struggling and kept helping until they were free. Whatever they did in response to my efforts to help was up to them. Whether I chose to help them or went on by without even stopping was what was up to me.

02

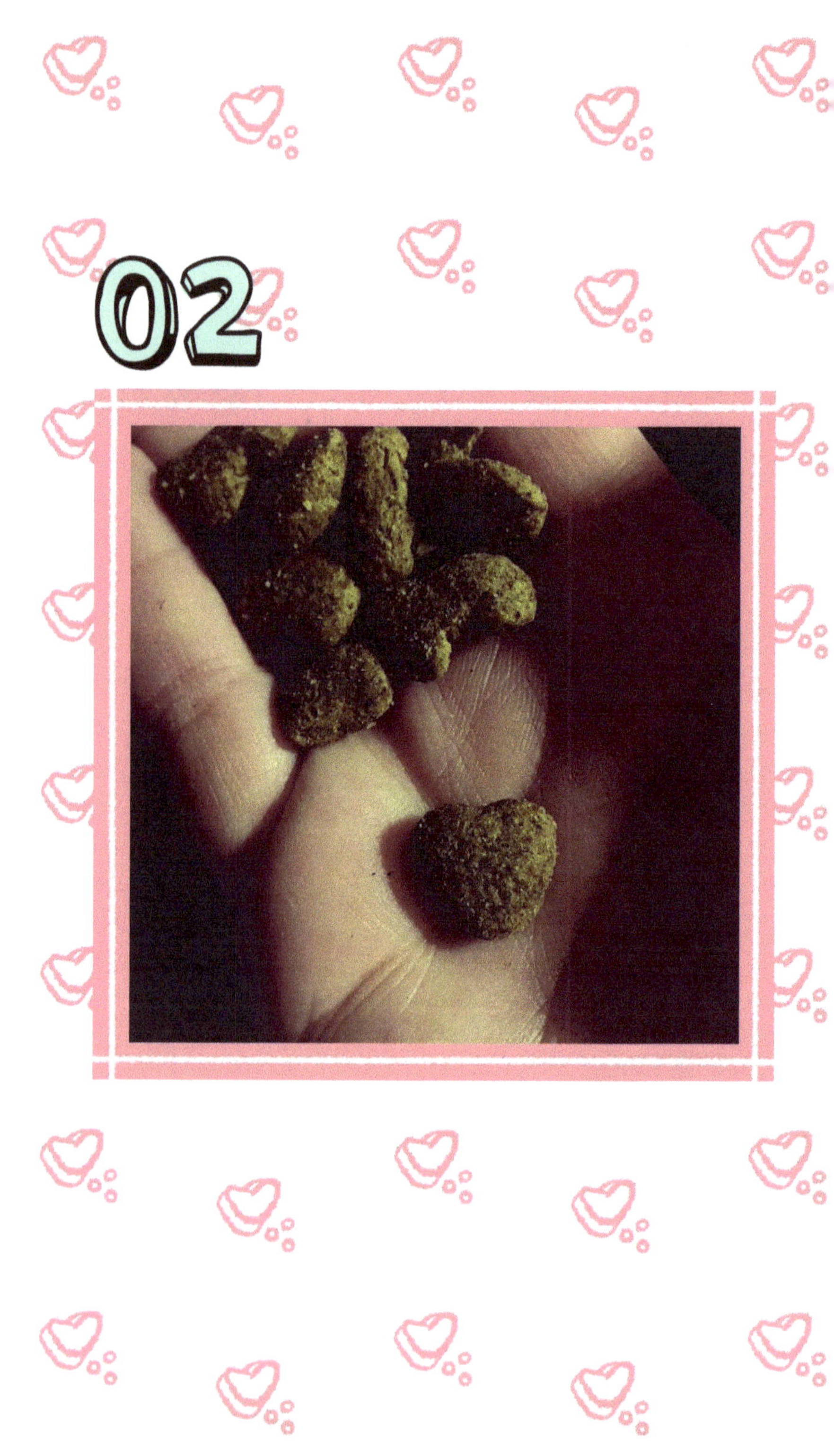

I filled my dog's bowl with dog food, and as I did, I noticed that some of the pieces looked like little hearts. I thought to myself, "Hmm, the dog can't tell the difference, so this must be made that way for me, the one who buys the dog food." A heart shape conveys love. It could mean healthy for the heart too. The manufacturer is trying to convince me that this is the dog food that I need to choose. It's subtle; it's tricky, it's subliminal advertising. Isn't that just the way of the world? Every advertisement, commercial, billboard, selfie, social media status, aren't they all trying so hard to convince us of something? Be aware and be vigilant. The world is working overtime to make you think something is better for you than it is. Sticking to God's ways and precepts is difficult, but in the end, it's what will feed you best and healthiest for your heart!

03

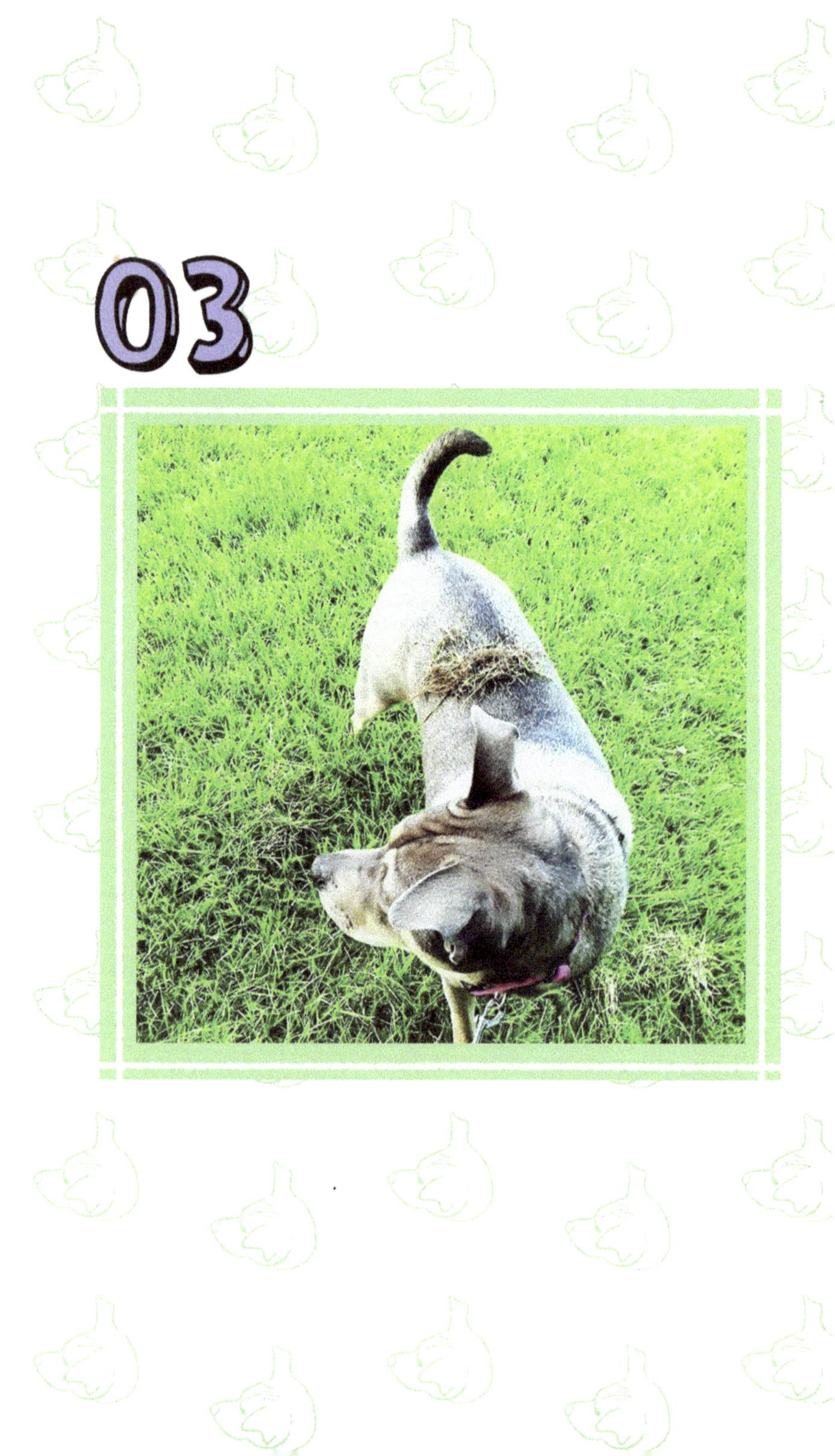

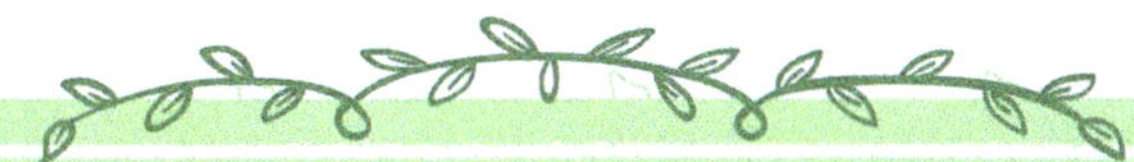

My dog Darcy likes to really kick up the grass after doing her "business." Today she kicked so hard that a big clump of grass landed on her back. She kept walking around as if all was utterly normal. She keeps me entertained, but don't we all do that? Don't we all have habits that eventually throw things onto our backs to carry that shouldn't be there? We walk around like everything is normal and can't see the ridiculousness of our actions. Still, everyone else can easily see what we carry. Isn't it always easier to see other people's stuff? This is why we need to be living in a community. We need to help each other. And like I did this morning, sometimes specifically help a brother or sister clean off that junk they have been carrying around for no good reason.

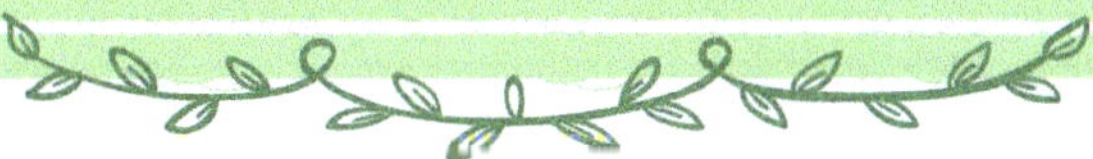

04

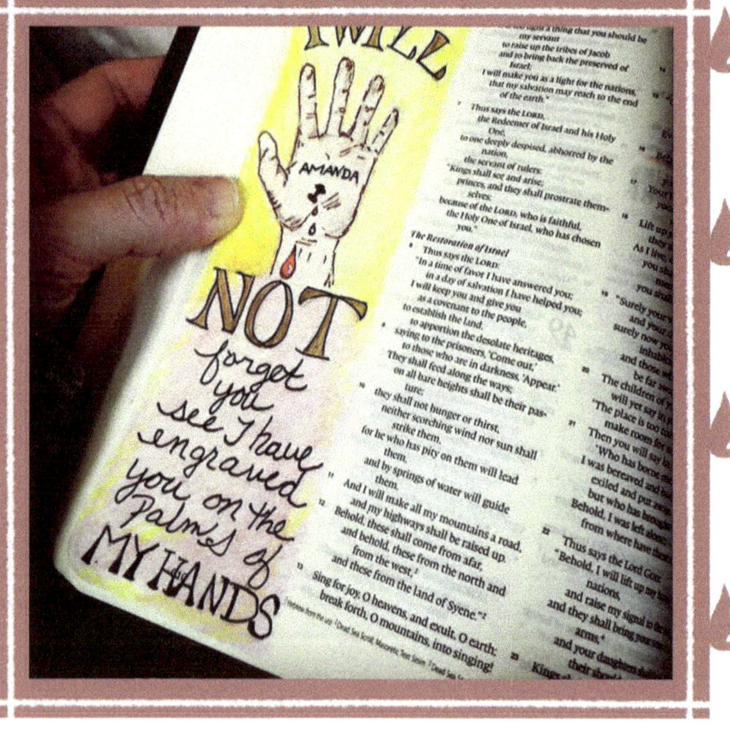
I WILL
NOT
forget you
see I have
engraved
you on the
palms of
MY HANDS
AMANDA

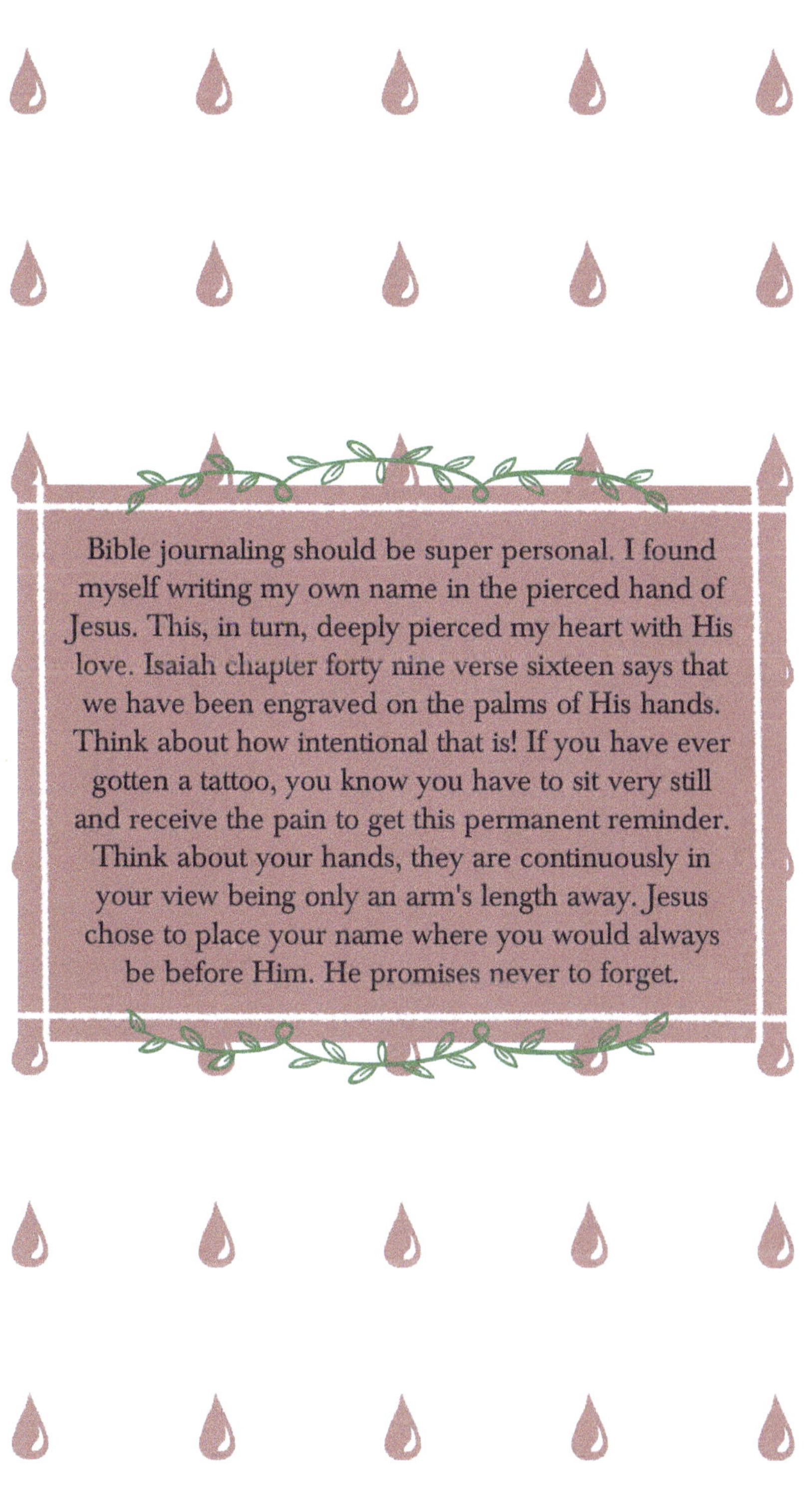

Bible journaling should be super personal. I found myself writing my own name in the pierced hand of Jesus. This, in turn, deeply pierced my heart with His love. Isaiah chapter forty nine verse sixteen says that we have been engraved on the palms of His hands. Think about how intentional that is! If you have ever gotten a tattoo, you know you have to sit very still and receive the pain to get this permanent reminder. Think about your hands, they are continuously in your view being only an arm's length away. Jesus chose to place your name where you would always be before Him. He promises never to forget.

05

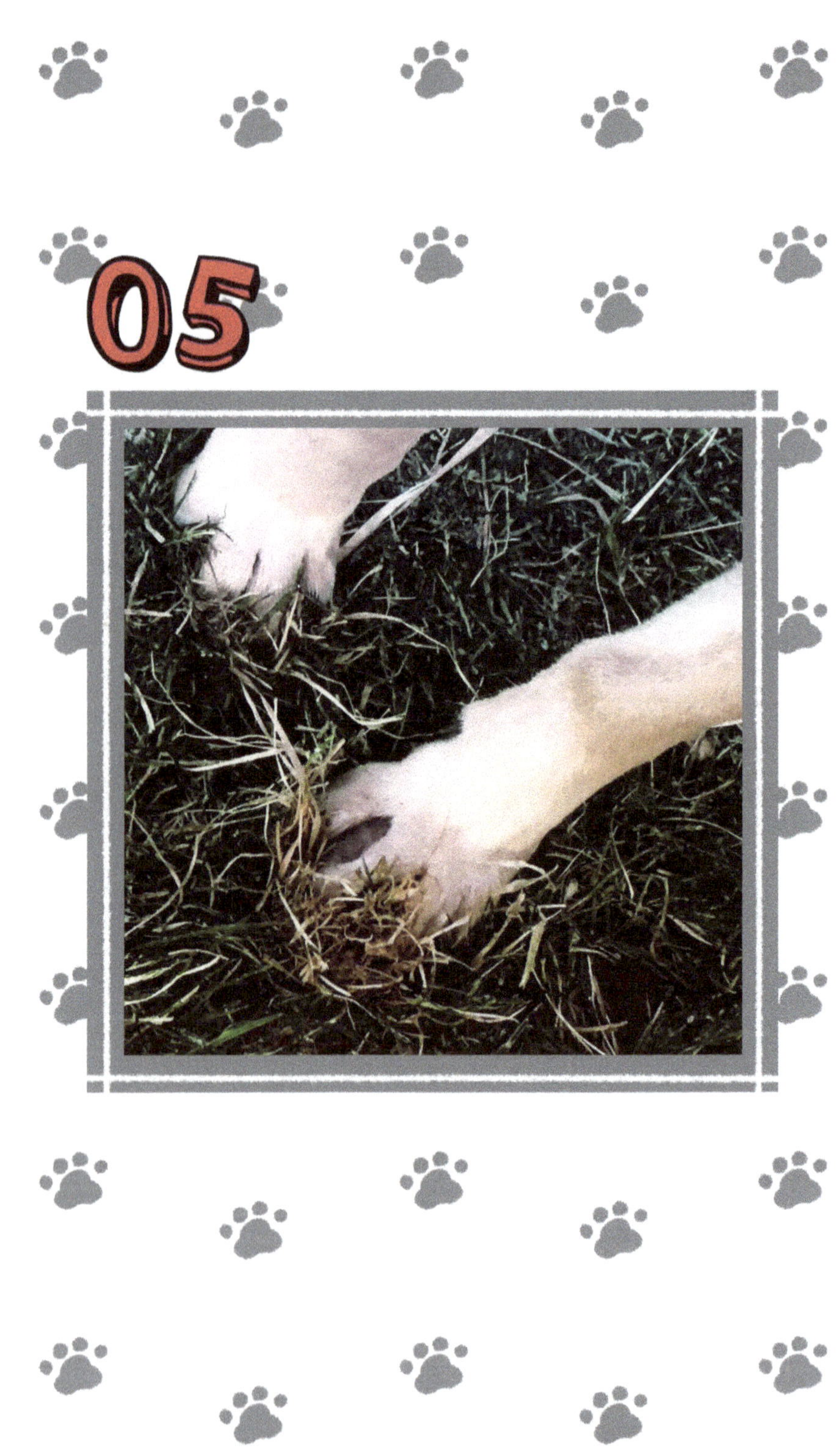

Does this look as dumb to you as it does to me? It's not only silly looking, but it's impractical and unnecessary. As I have told you before, Darcy is a rescue dog. She hates having her nails clipped more than any dog I have had. Although it's dangerous that nails break off on their own, the Vet said it is okay only to stress her out and do them when they get scary bad. So because she is so afraid, I wait until times like now. Here's the reason I share this: if she would get over her fear and regularly do what is right for her, she would be able to avoid picking up unwanted things. It's as if the clumps of mud and grass represent the additional anxieties and wrong thinking that come from operating out of a place of fear. Still, she would rather carry all that ridiculous stuff around than trust her master to help her. It's a work in progress. She has gotten a lot better, but we still have work to do. In the meantime, please note that she cannot get that stuff off herself. She needs me to bend down and lovingly clean it off of her. As I did so this morning, I felt the gentle, loving presence of my Father bending down over me. He is lovingly cleaning me off in my ridiculous places. It's a work in progress, but I have gotten a lot better too.

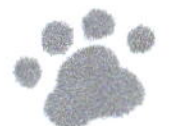
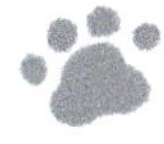
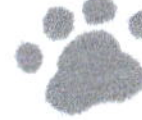

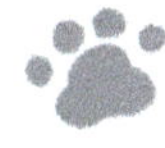

06

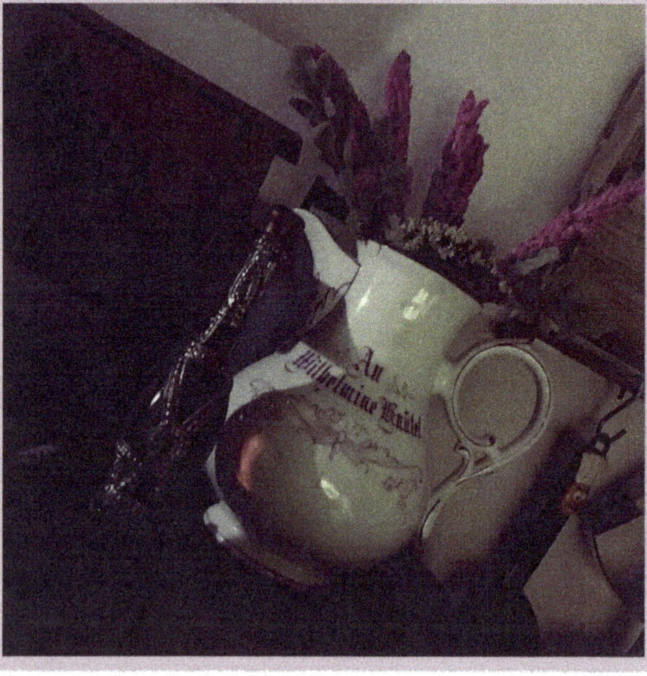

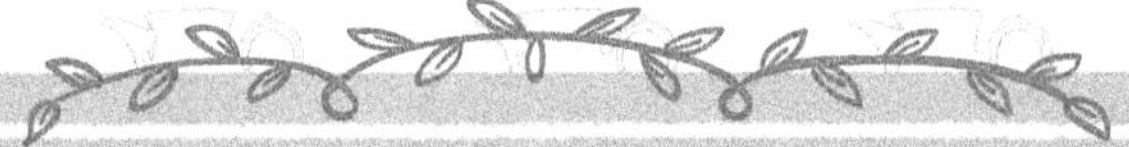

Early morning light from the other room made its way into the dark kitchen this morning. It passed through the bottle of Italian vinegar and left a mark on the pitcher. Light penetrates. Light passes through things. Light leaves an impression. Light illumines and changes the appearance of things. It comes in waves and has a frequency. It reflects. It expands and radiates and bends. It carries energy and momentum and interacts with others. It grows things and warms us. God created light and used it to describe Jesus. Light expels the darkness. Some everyday words aren't ordinary at all; they have just been overused and under-appreciated.

07

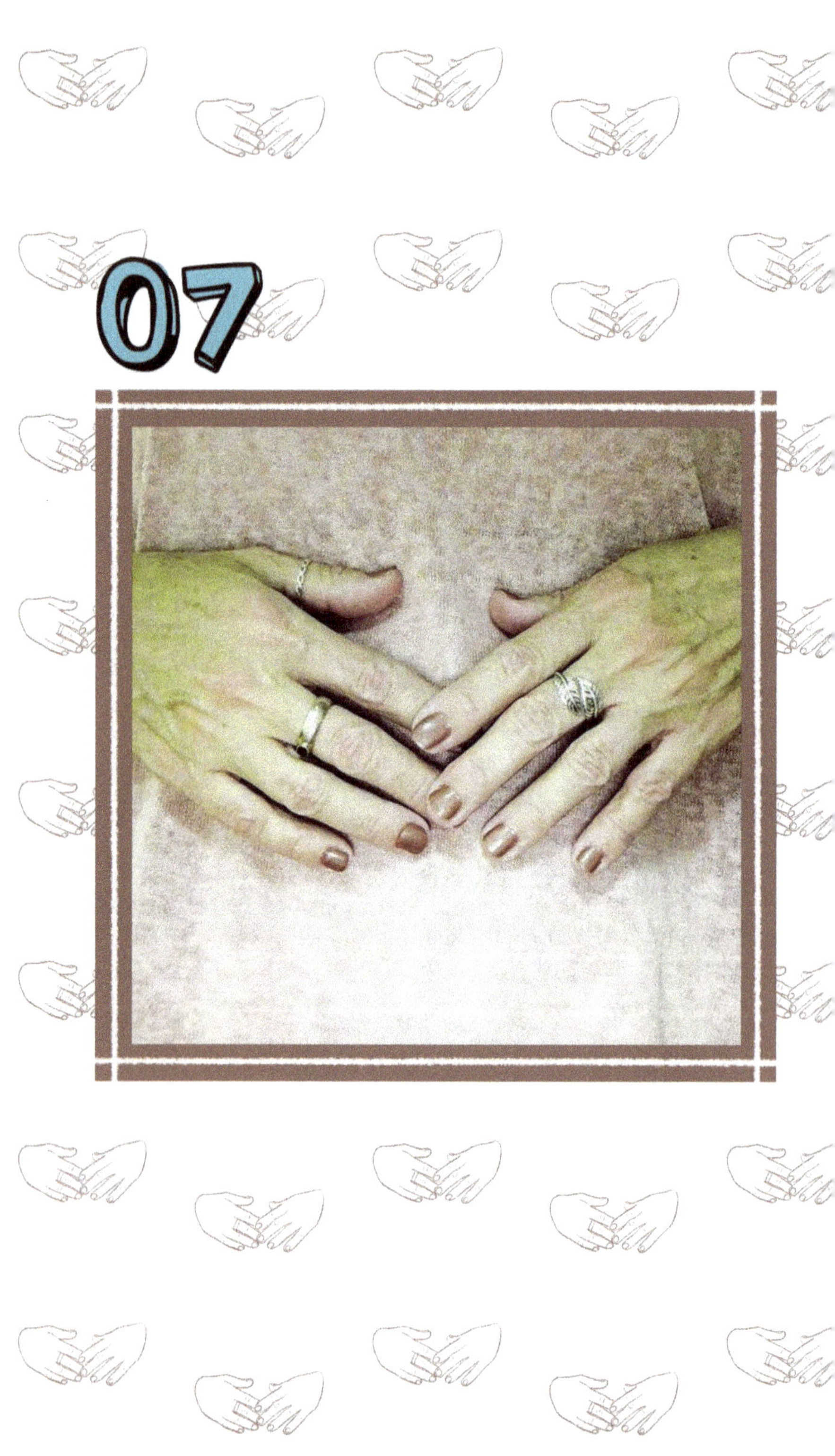

Fun fact: I never liked my hands even when they were young hands. I have big knuckles, short nails, and there is always a cut on a finger or two. Now they are older, and they work harder. Still, these are the hands that care for people. These are the hands that paint and sew and knit and crochet. These are the hands that prepare food for my family, and they are the hands that make my home welcoming to others.

These are the hands that help me write my heart down on paper, and these are the hands that I use to express my worship to God. These hands wipe tears away; they move around as I speak and bring my stories to life! Before my daughter's wedding, my dear friend, who had no idea how I felt about my hands, insisted on blessing me and getting me a manicure. As she loved me and blessed me with her beautiful, generous heart, I heard God whisper, "Your hands are beautiful! I made them do what you are doing with them, not to look a certain way; you must understand what is truly beautiful my child." With one gesture of kindness came such deep love that touched my heart and healed ancient wounds that I never knew where there. Surround yourself with Godly friends and let them bless you every once in a while.

08

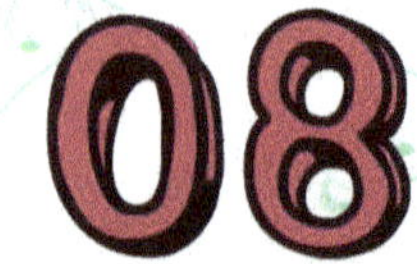

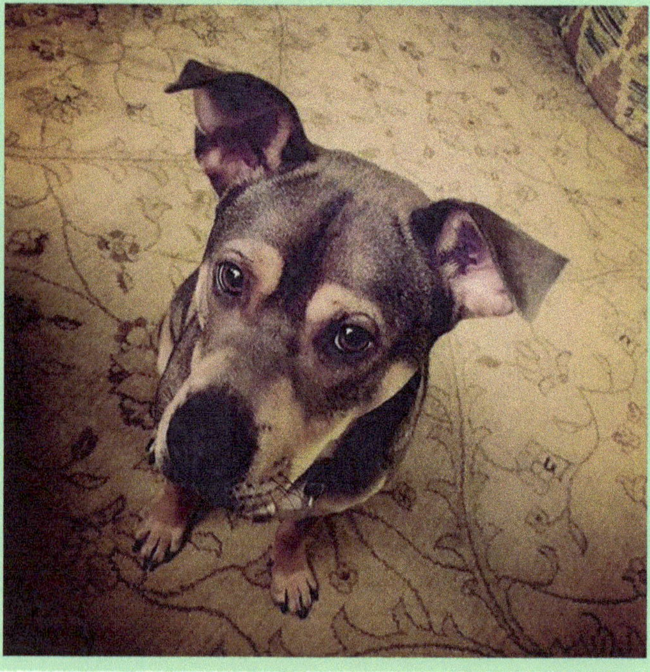

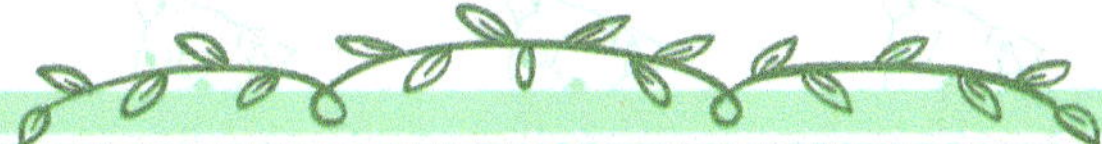

God brought this beautiful rescue dog into my life. He has used her to help me to understand the degree of patience and tender-heartedness that He has for me. I have loved her unconditionally through bad behaviors and disobedience. I have poured myself out to her, bent down to comfort her, spoken softly so as not to overwhelm her. I have set aside my feelings and desires to assure her and through consistency of character, I have won her trust and her love. She sits with me this morning as I worship God, she is familiar with my falling on my knees or my face and also with my climbing onto the nearest chair to praise Him. She is no longer confused by my tears of sorrow and joy. She sits waiting for me to move, and when I do, she follows until I settle into a new place. She depends on me for food and water and shelter and love. Who knew that when my son begged me to adopt her that the Father would use her to show me His amazing heart towards me? Be open to our Father, who has chosen us as one of His own. He longs to set us free from the chaos of the life we led and bring us into a place of freedom and rest with Him.

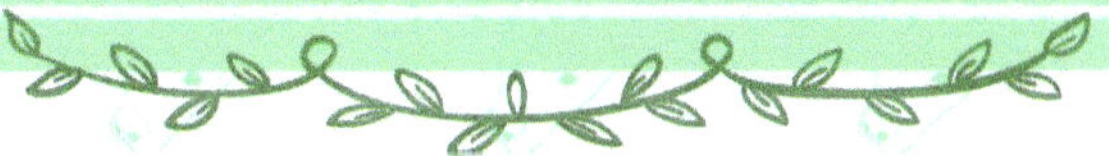

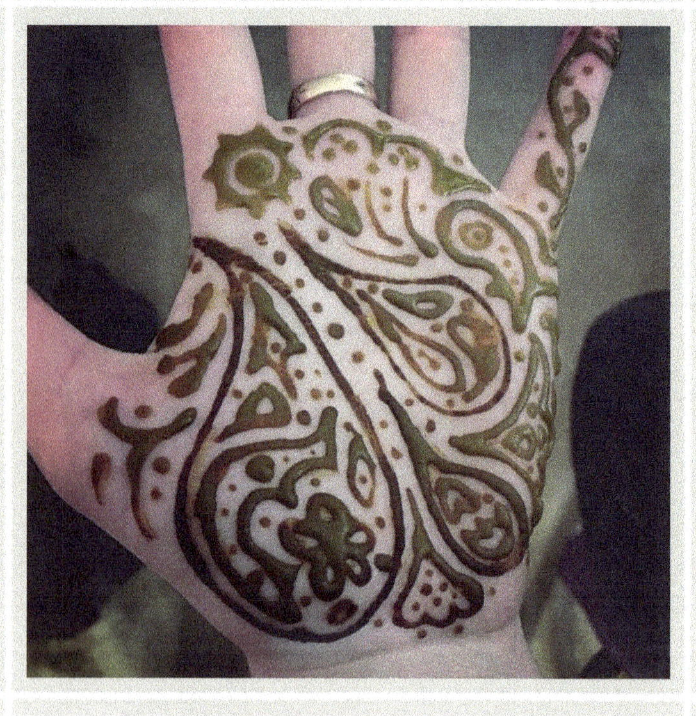

Henna has this beautiful smell of eucalyptus. As Mary Elizabeth skillfully prepared it, the scent wafted all around us. I was quietly aware as we, this band of women, laughed and talked (mostly giggled). I was mindful of the truth of several scriptures. As we sat on couches sharing blankets, watching comedies, tears streaming down our faces, the scriptures just kept coming into my heart. Together we were a pleasing aroma to Jesus. We were written on the palm of His Hand. As we made our way through the night as this gathering of strong women, this family in Christ, I realized how our love and laughter pleased Him. How this was all from Him: that God had made us better as a group, to be better as encouragers, as sisters, as a family!

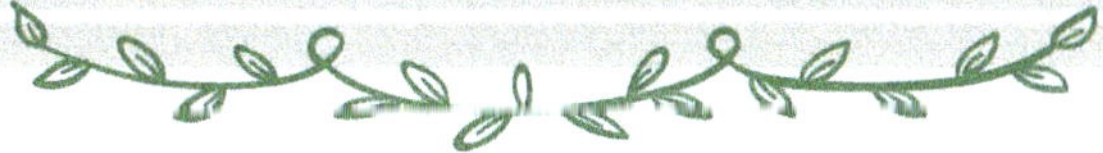

10

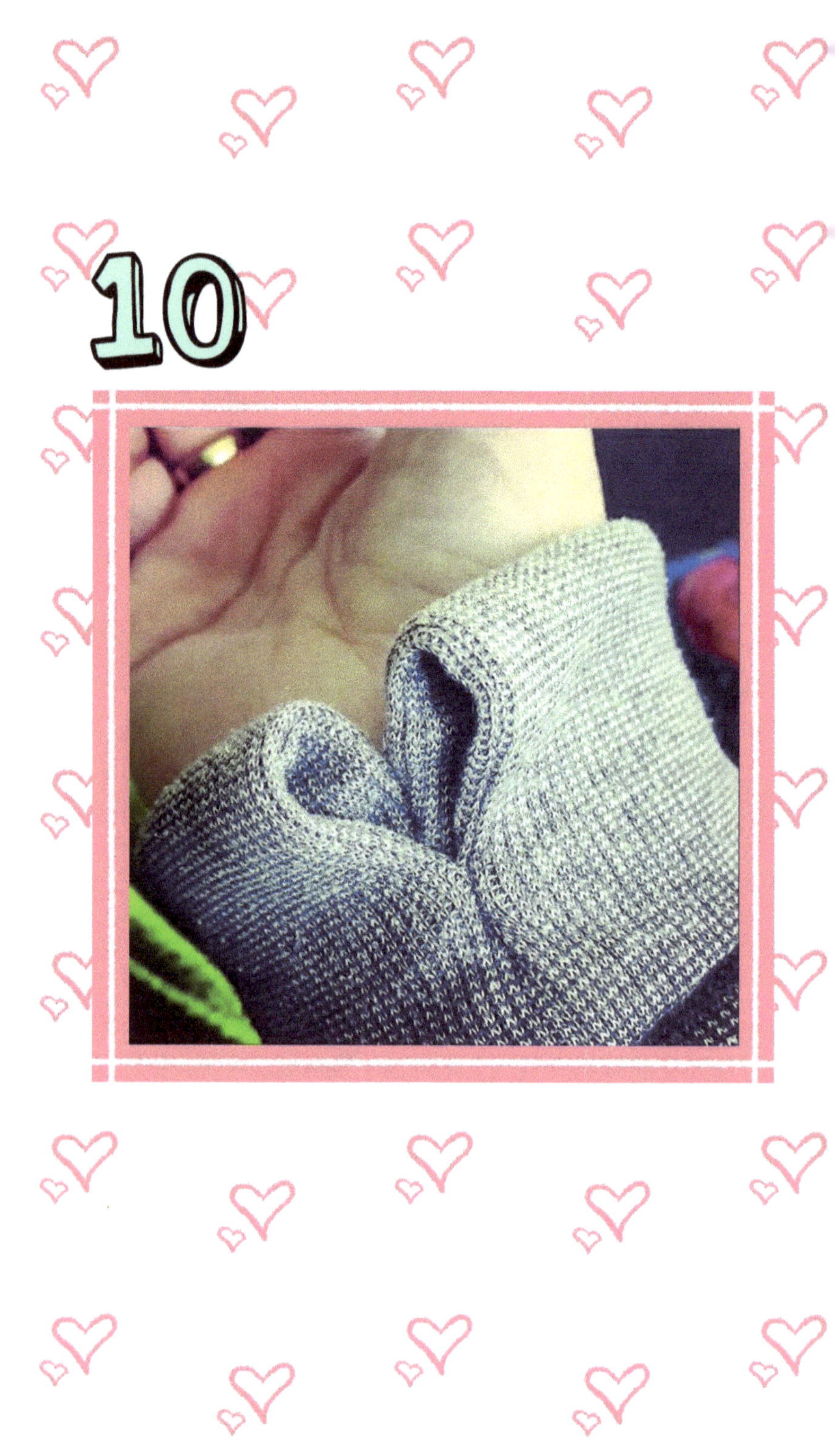

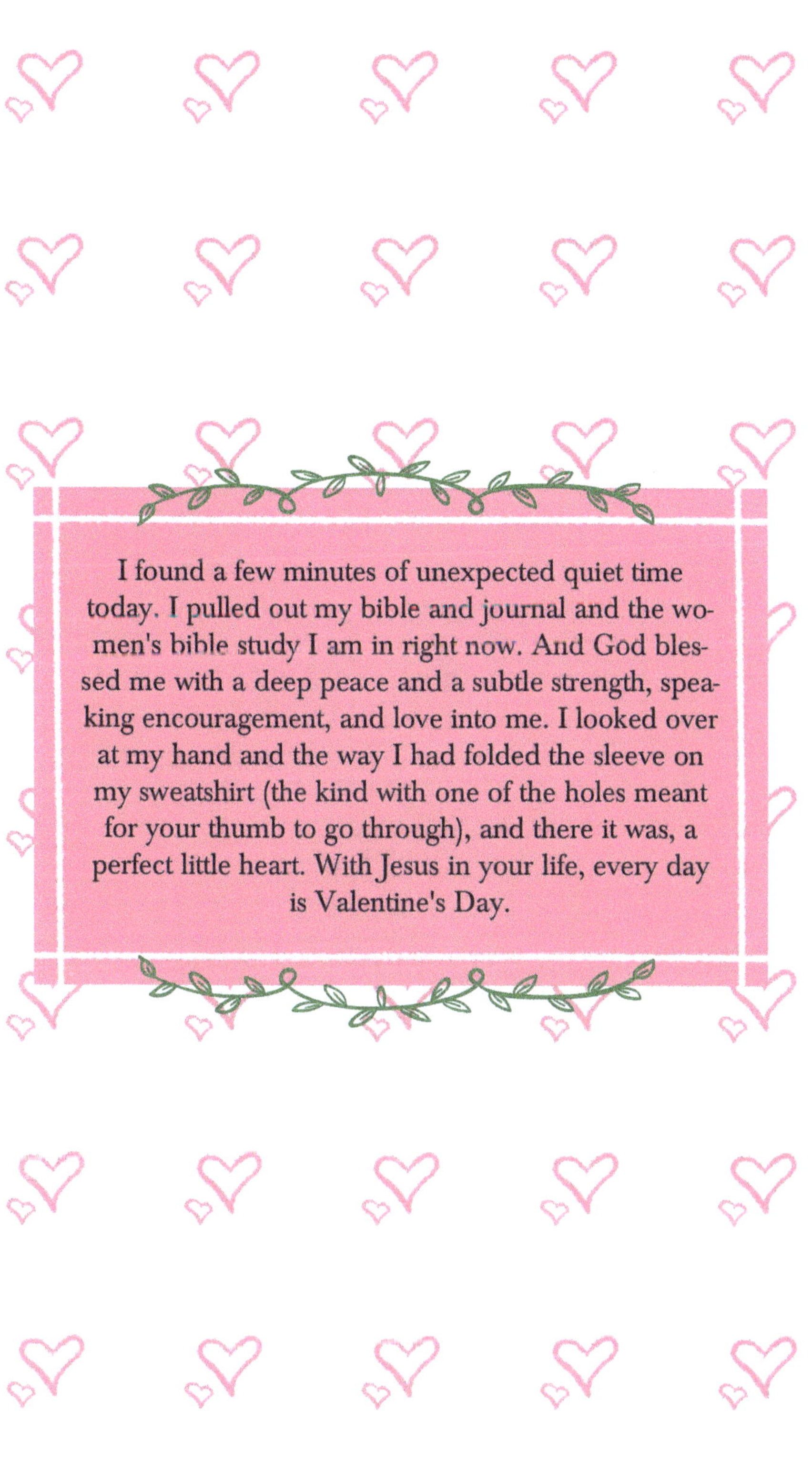

I found a few minutes of unexpected quiet time today. I pulled out my bible and journal and the women's bible study I am in right now. And God blessed me with a deep peace and a subtle strength, speaking encouragement, and love into me. I looked over at my hand and the way I had folded the sleeve on my sweatshirt (the kind with one of the holes meant for your thumb to go through), and there it was, a perfect little heart. With Jesus in your life, every day is Valentine's Day.

11

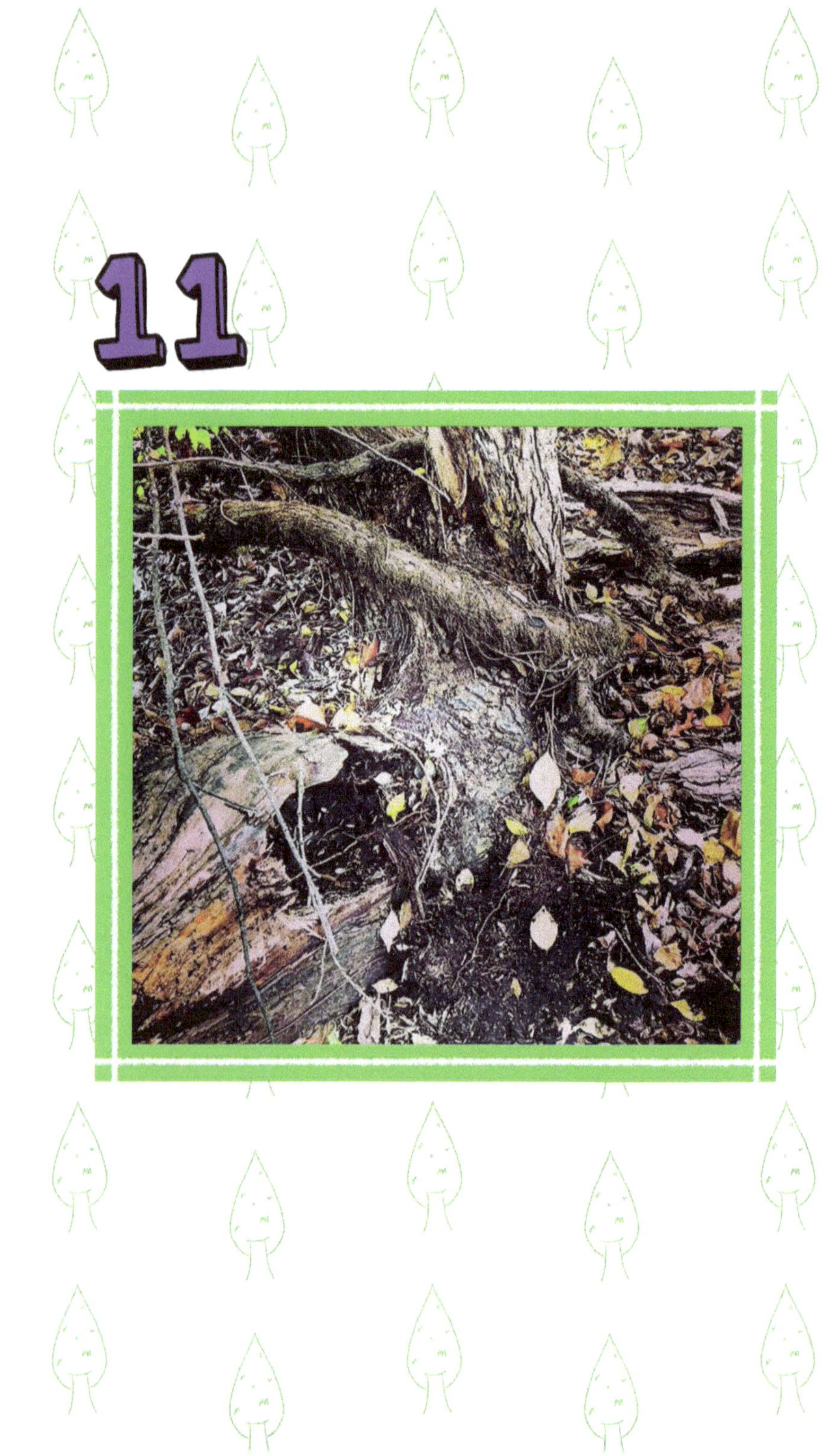

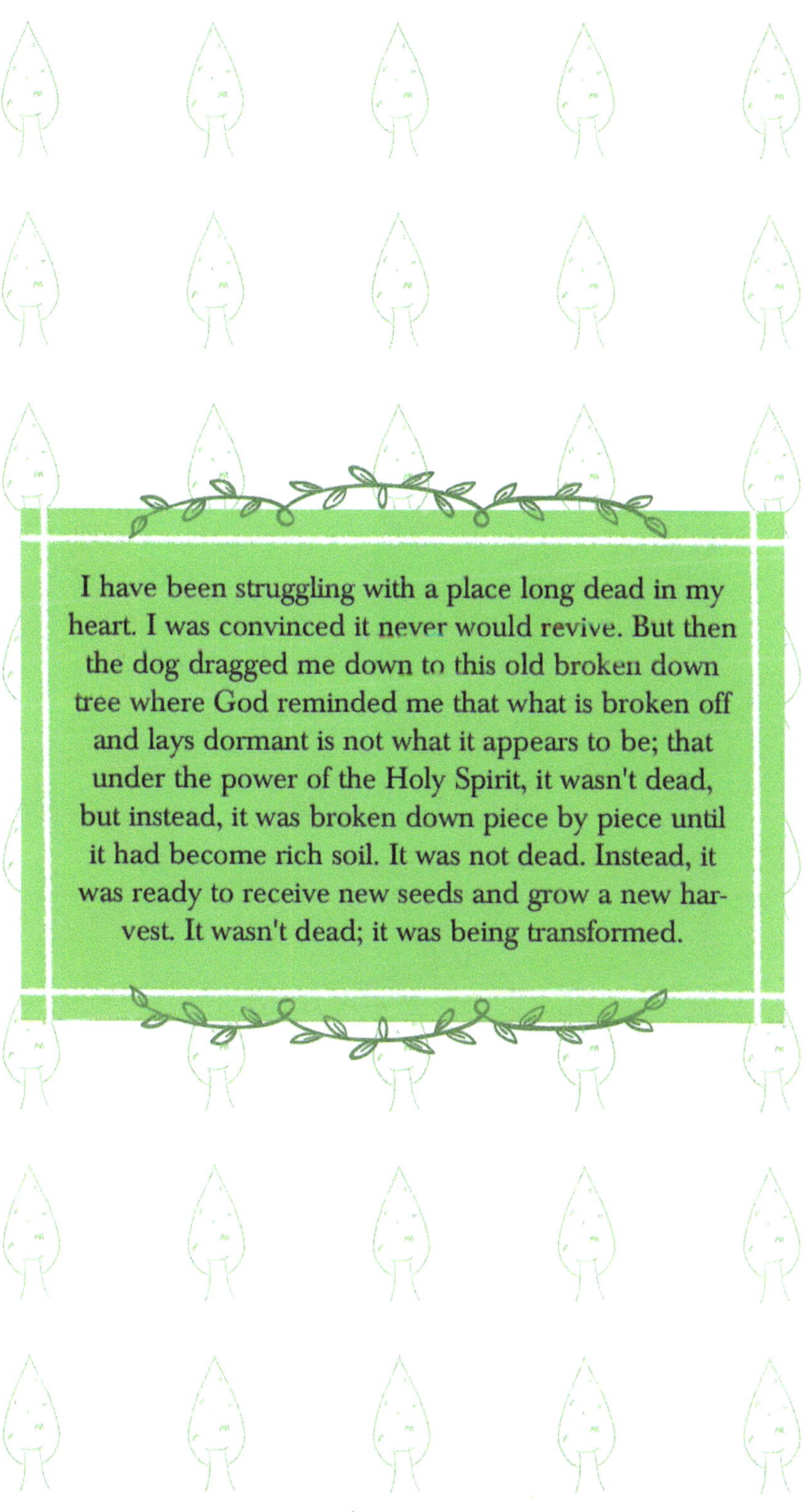

I have been struggling with a place long dead in my heart. I was convinced it never would revive. But then the dog dragged me down to this old broken down tree where God reminded me that what is broken off and lays dormant is not what it appears to be; that under the power of the Holy Spirit, it wasn't dead, but instead, it was broken down piece by piece until it had become rich soil. It was not dead. Instead, it was ready to receive new seeds and grow a new harvest. It wasn't dead; it was being transformed.

12

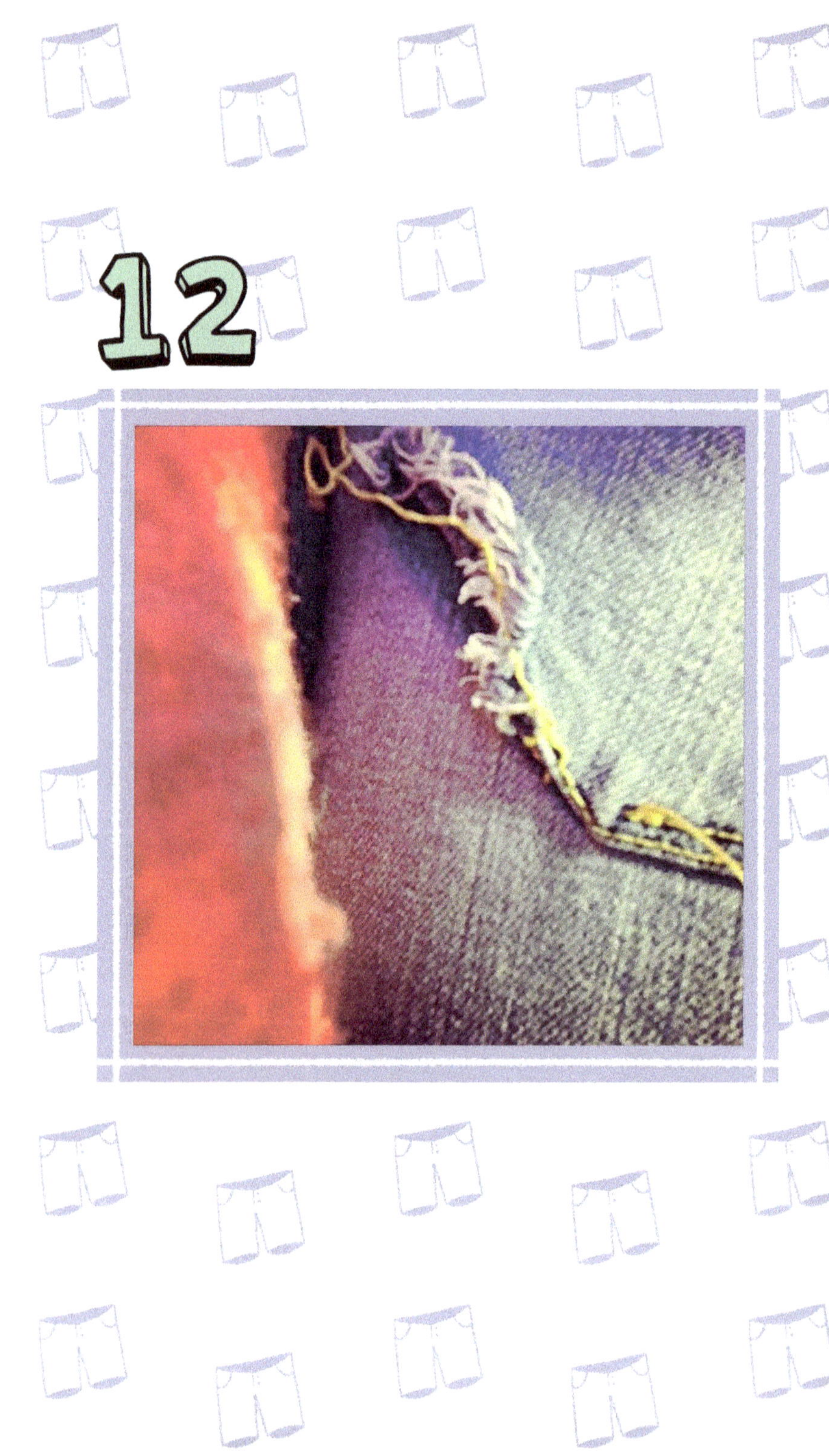

I have on a pair of my favorite jeans. The back right-hand pocket has a hole at the bottom. I could sew it, but have never taken the time to do it. I know it's there every time I put the pants on, but here's the thing, I keep putting my phone in that pocket out of habit. Without thinking, I put my phone in the pocket (over and over again all day). Within seconds, it falls to the ground. Sometimes the most significant truths are wrapped up in the simplest packages. How many times do we know something is broken in our hearts, but we don't take the time to mend it? How often do we do things out of habit without thinking, without seeing the obvious outcome of our actions? If I keep this up, one of these days, my phone will break. If we keep going on with broken hearts, whatever we try to put in them will eventually break also. God speaks in everyday things. So guess what? Today I am going to sew the pocket.

13

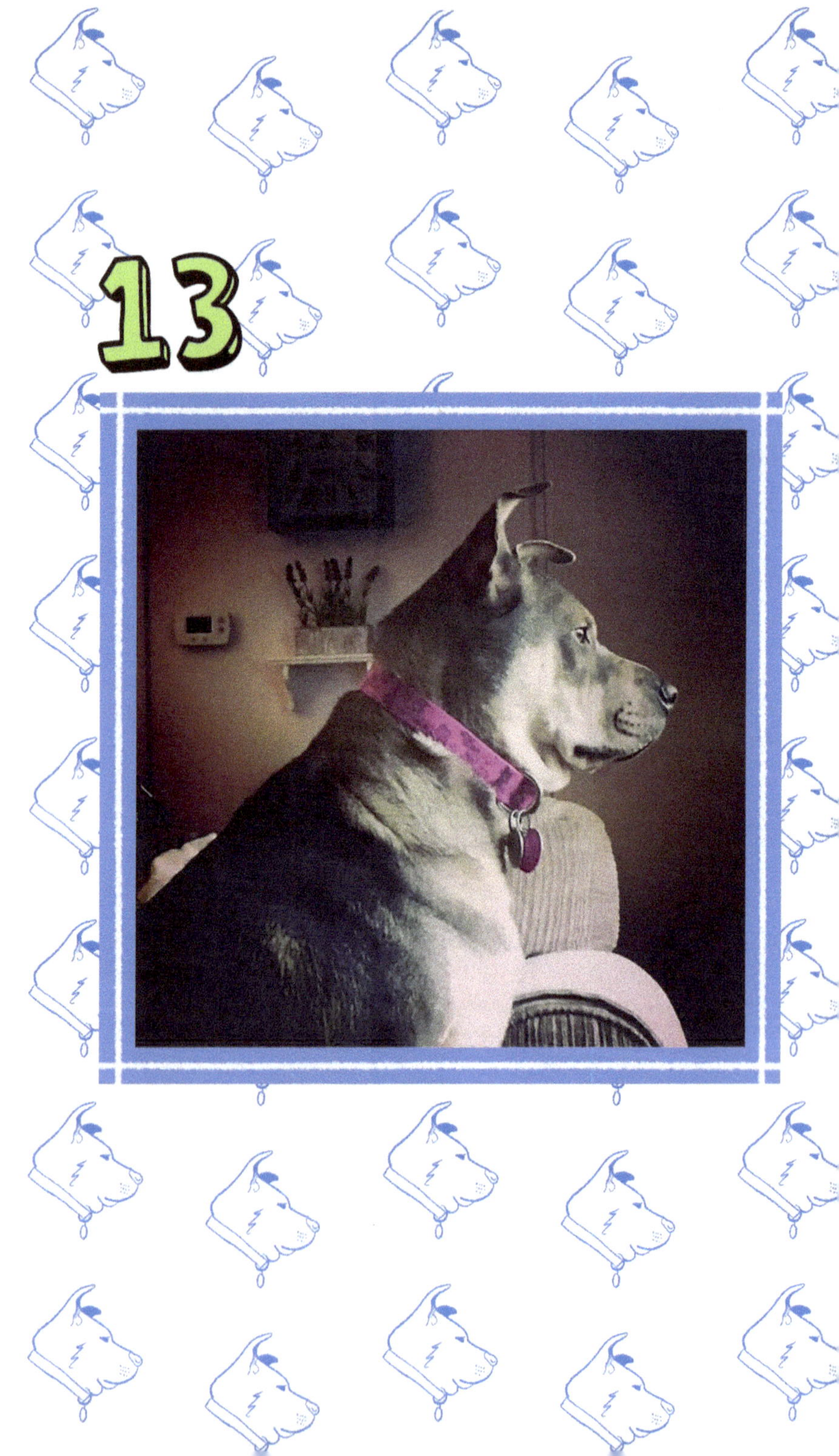

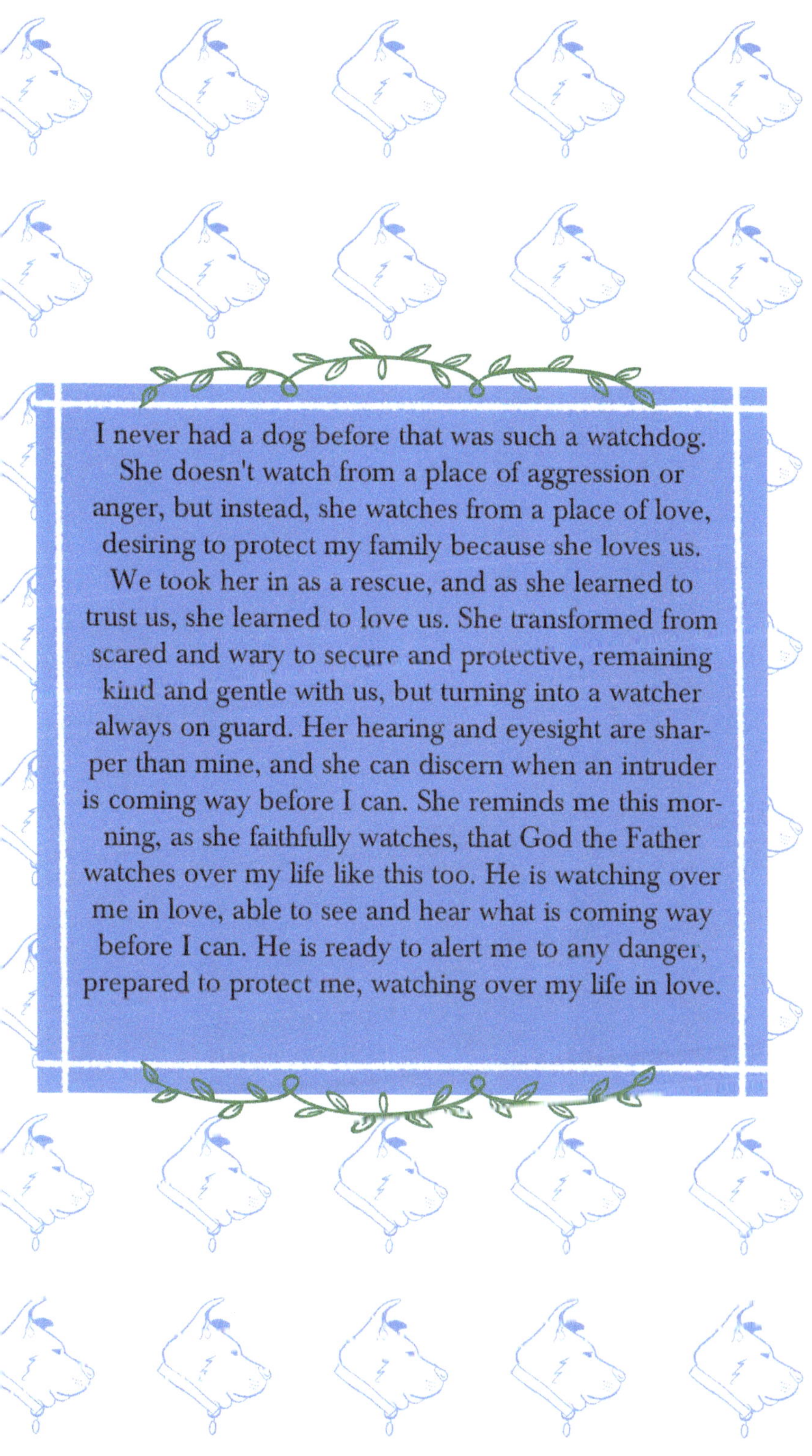

I never had a dog before that was such a watchdog. She doesn't watch from a place of aggression or anger, but instead, she watches from a place of love, desiring to protect my family because she loves us. We took her in as a rescue, and as she learned to trust us, she learned to love us. She transformed from scared and wary to secure and protective, remaining kind and gentle with us, but turning into a watcher always on guard. Her hearing and eyesight are sharper than mine, and she can discern when an intruder is coming way before I can. She reminds me this morning, as she faithfully watches, that God the Father watches over my life like this too. He is watching over me in love, able to see and hear what is coming way before I can. He is ready to alert me to any danger, prepared to protect me, watching over my life in love.

14

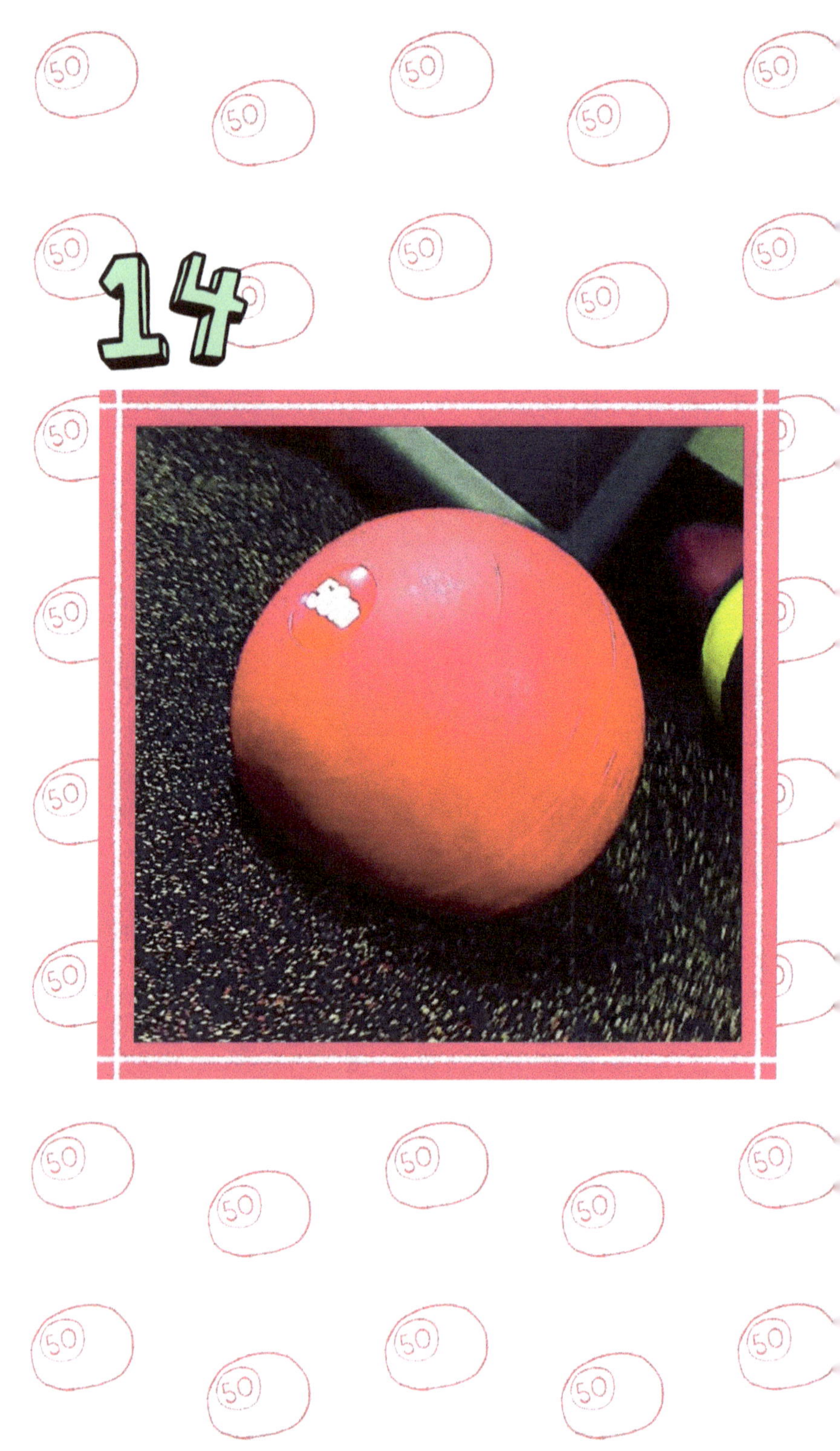

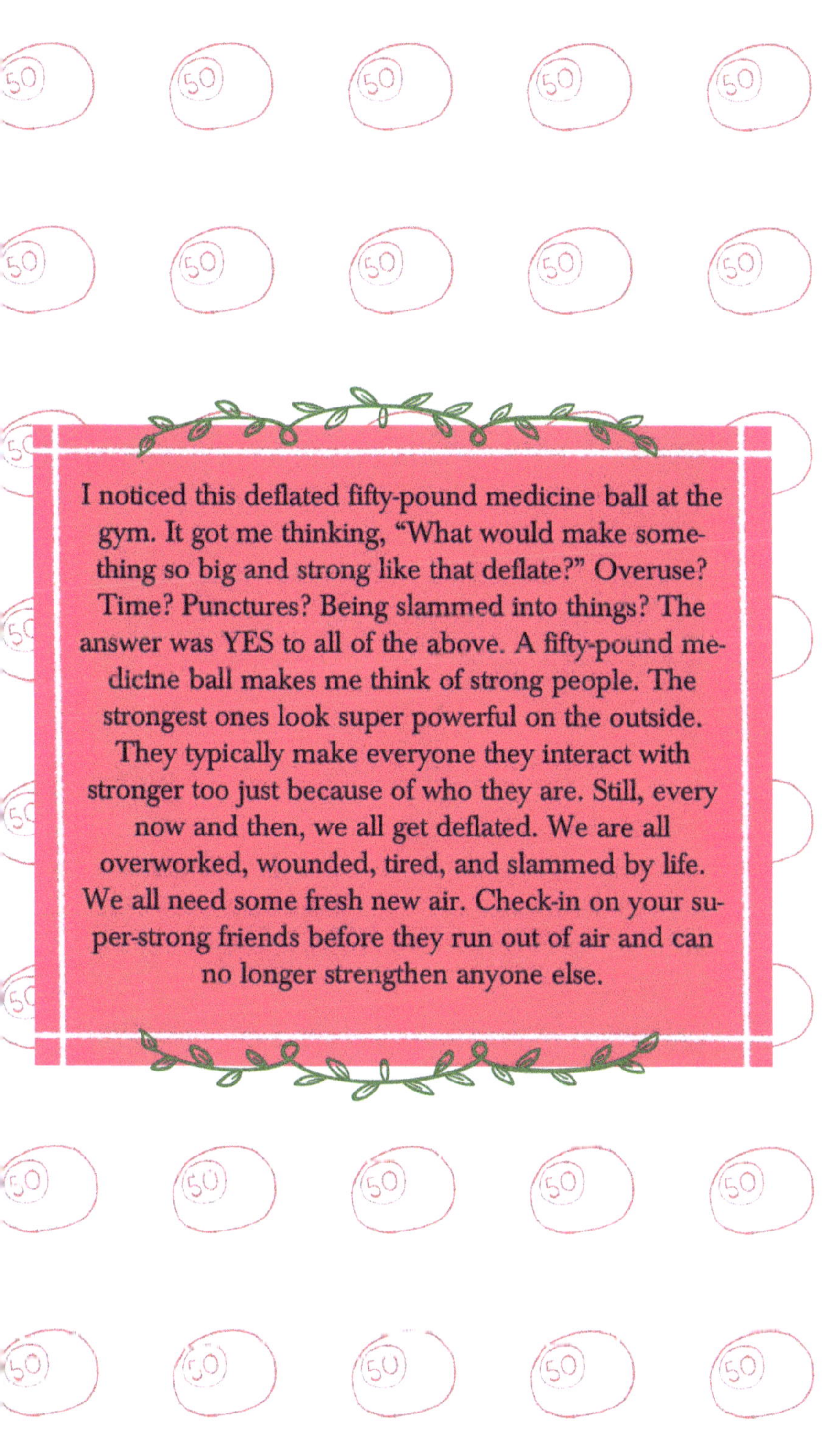

I noticed this deflated fifty-pound medicine ball at the gym. It got me thinking, "What would make something so big and strong like that deflate?" Overuse? Time? Punctures? Being slammed into things? The answer was YES to all of the above. A fifty-pound medicine ball makes me think of strong people. The strongest ones look super powerful on the outside. They typically make everyone they interact with stronger too just because of who they are. Still, every now and then, we all get deflated. We are all overworked, wounded, tired, and slammed by life. We all need some fresh new air. Check-in on your super-strong friends before they run out of air and can no longer strengthen anyone else.

15

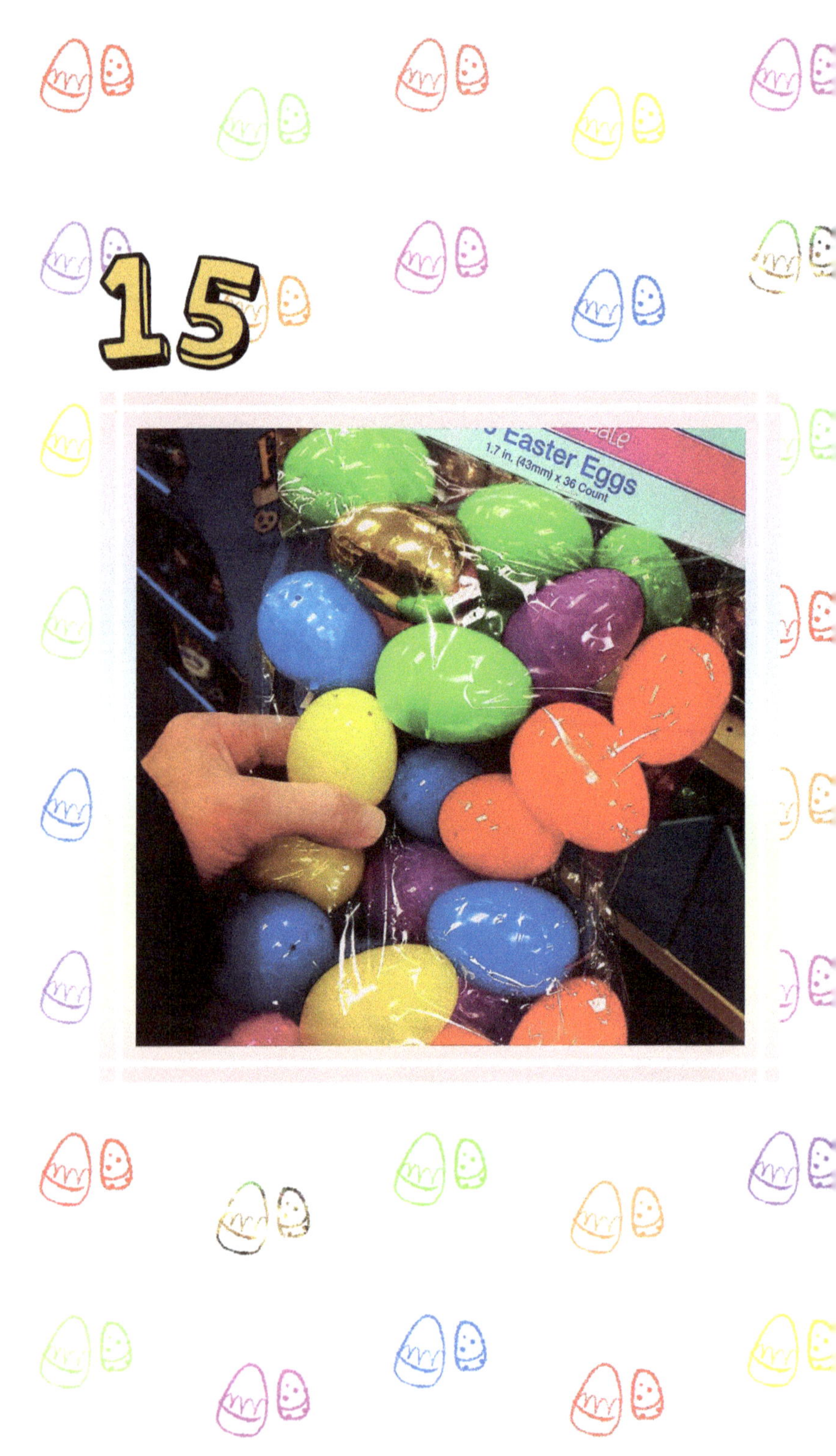

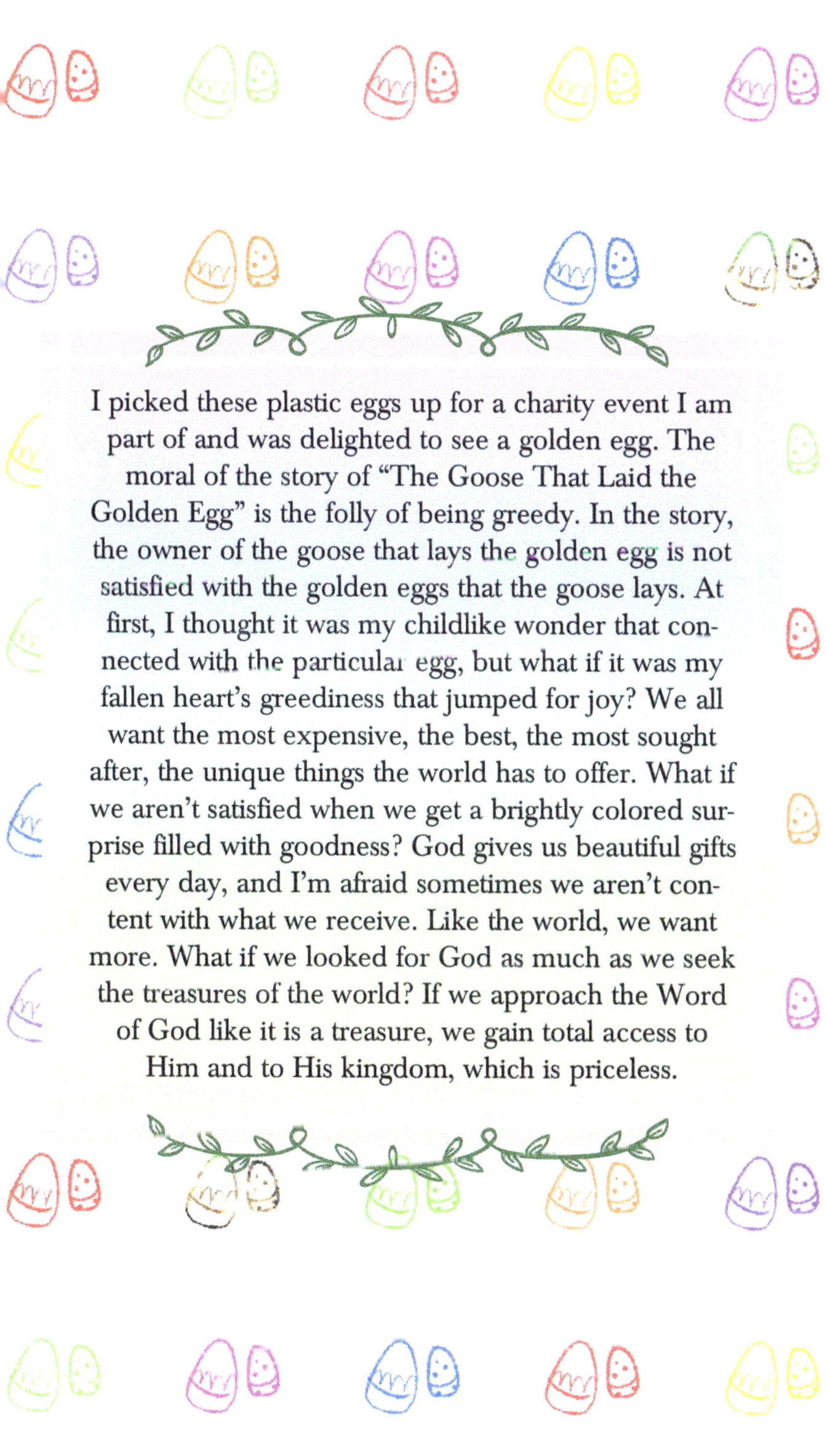

I picked these plastic eggs up for a charity event I am part of and was delighted to see a golden egg. The moral of the story of "The Goose That Laid the Golden Egg" is the folly of being greedy. In the story, the owner of the goose that lays the golden egg is not satisfied with the golden eggs that the goose lays. At first, I thought it was my childlike wonder that connected with the particular egg, but what if it was my fallen heart's greediness that jumped for joy? We all want the most expensive, the best, the most sought after, the unique things the world has to offer. What if we aren't satisfied when we get a brightly colored surprise filled with goodness? God gives us beautiful gifts every day, and I'm afraid sometimes we aren't content with what we receive. Like the world, we want more. What if we looked for God as much as we seek the treasures of the world? If we approach the Word of God like it is a treasure, we gain total access to Him and to His kingdom, which is priceless.

16

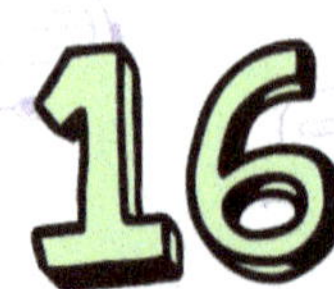

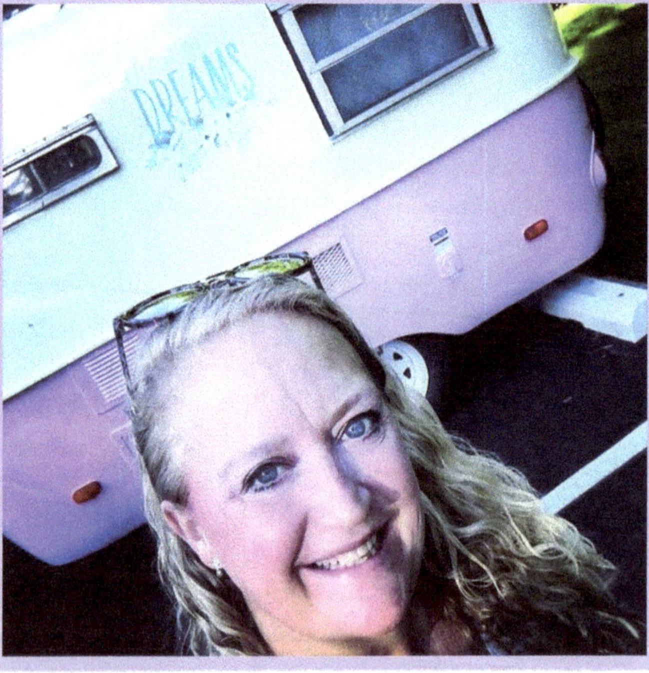

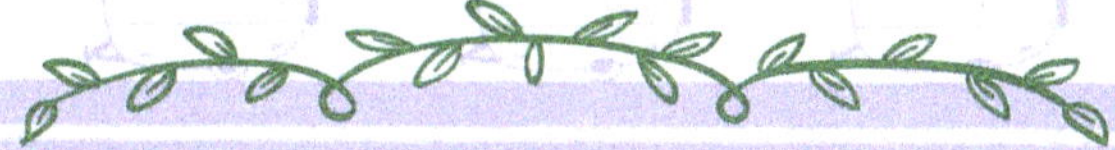

I posted this cute little camper the day I first saw it. Every time I walked the dog or drove by, I saw it. It was parked right at the edge of where I live. It said "Chase Your Dreams" on it. This camper was a personal message for me, wrapped up in one beautiful little package. The camper was pink and teal, one color representing my calling to minister to women, one my favorite color. The message to chase my dreams reminded me that my creativity and my interests and talents would help me to accomplish my ministry. It is at the very edge of where I have my home reminding me that each of us has an area of reach, of ministry right where we are already living. It is just far enough away that I have to make an effort to get to it, but just close enough that I can see it and tell what it is. I had been praying about all of this asking God lots of questions, and it seems He placed some answers right within my sight. I also gave God back a dream recently and asked Him to tell me if it was my dream or His dream for me and asked explicitly, "Should I chase my dream?"

17

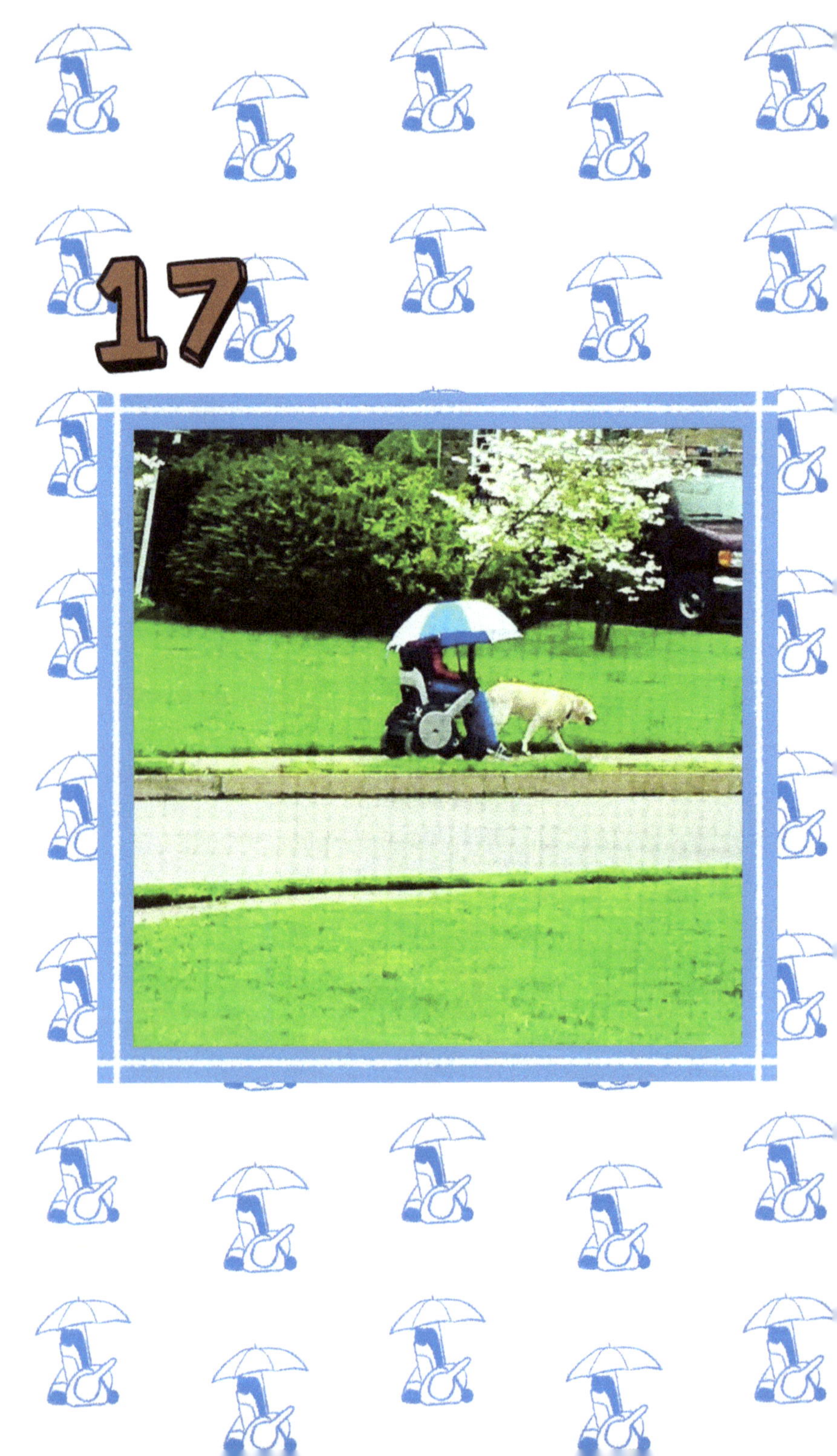

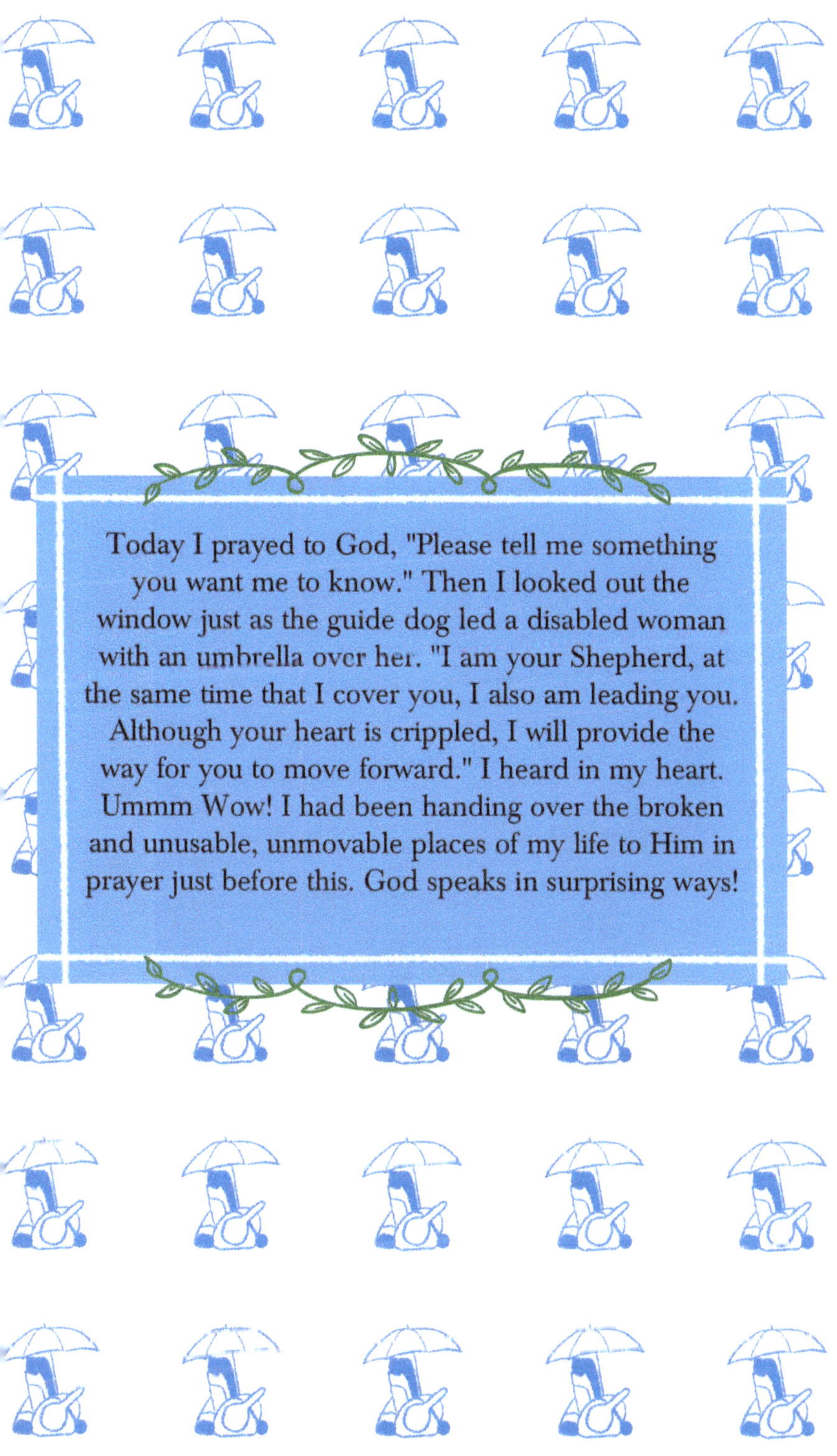

Today I prayed to God, "Please tell me something you want me to know." Then I looked out the window just as the guide dog led a disabled woman with an umbrella over her. "I am your Shepherd, at the same time that I cover you, I also am leading you. Although your heart is crippled, I will provide the way for you to move forward." I heard in my heart. Ummm Wow! I had been handing over the broken and unusable, unmovable places of my life to Him in prayer just before this. God speaks in surprising ways!

18

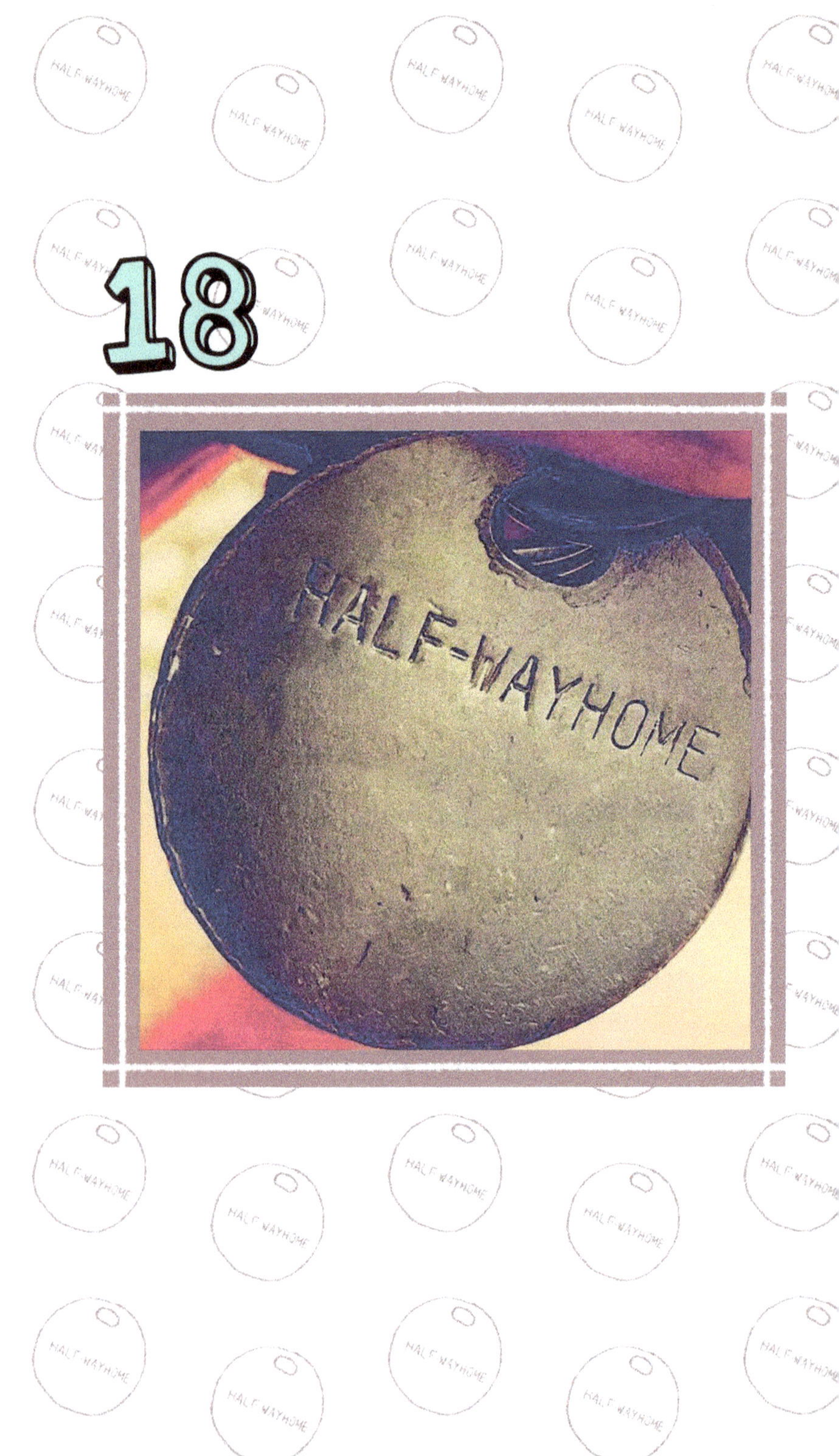

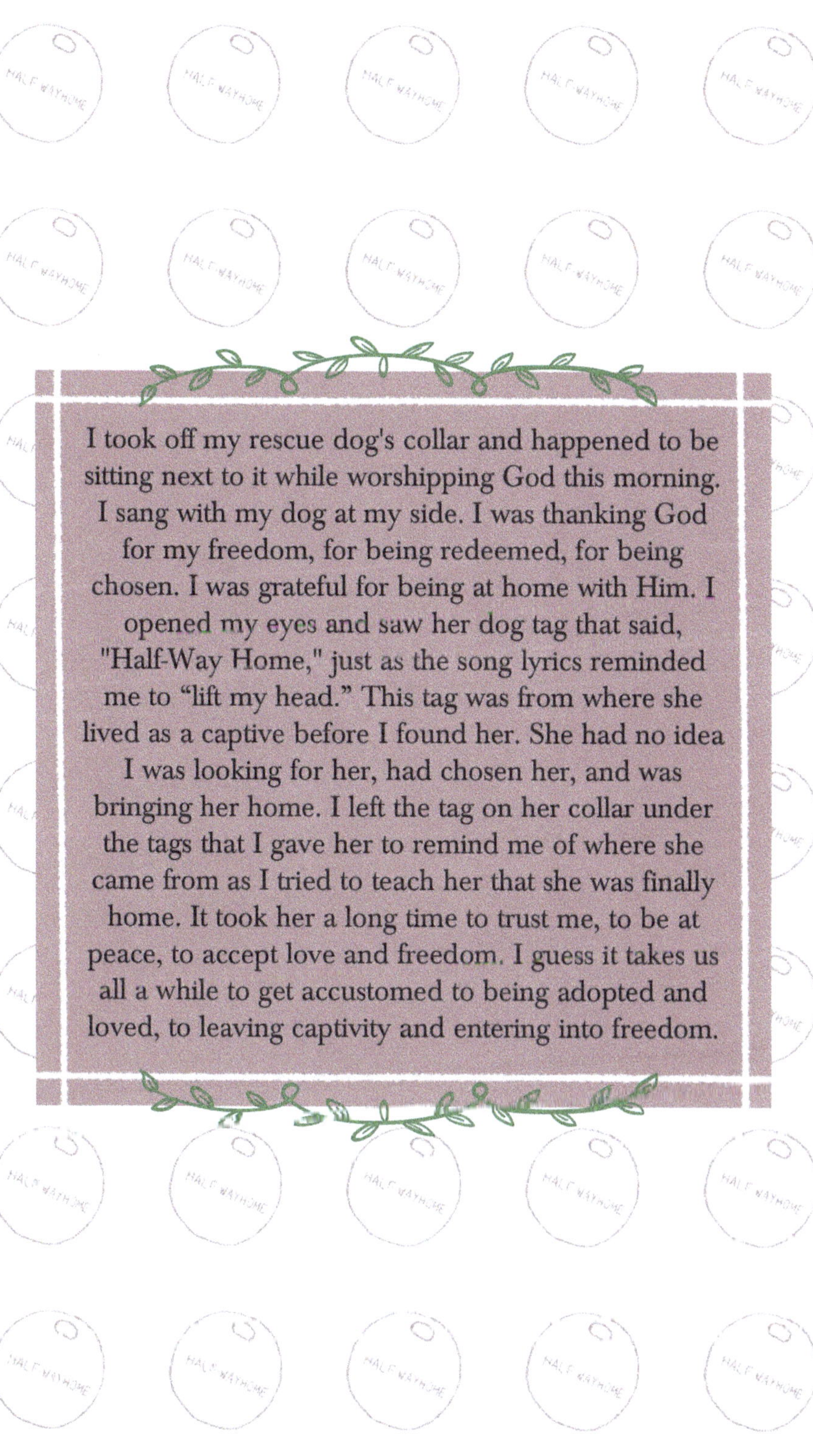

I took off my rescue dog's collar and happened to be sitting next to it while worshipping God this morning. I sang with my dog at my side. I was thanking God for my freedom, for being redeemed, for being chosen. I was grateful for being at home with Him. I opened my eyes and saw her dog tag that said, "Half-Way Home," just as the song lyrics reminded me to "lift my head." This tag was from where she lived as a captive before I found her. She had no idea I was looking for her, had chosen her, and was bringing her home. I left the tag on her collar under the tags that I gave her to remind me of where she came from as I tried to teach her that she was finally home. It took her a long time to trust me, to be at peace, to accept love and freedom. I guess it takes us all a while to get accustomed to being adopted and loved, to leaving captivity and entering into freedom.

19

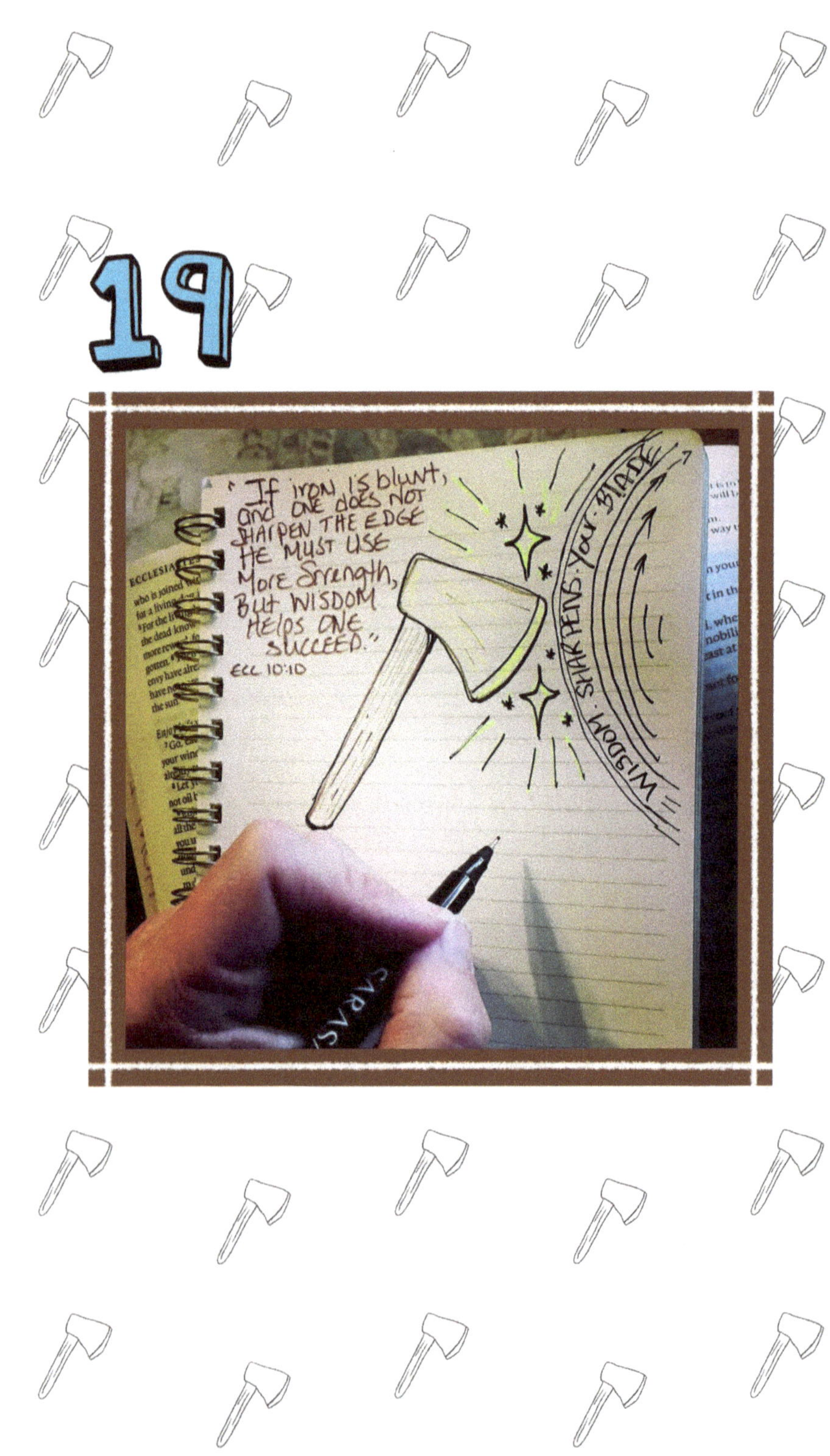

"If iron is blunt, and one does not sharpen the edge he must use more strength, but wisdom helps one succeed."
ECC 10:10
WISDOM SHARPENS YOUR BLADE

Wisdom sharpens your blade according to the bible, "If iron is blunt and one does not sharpen the edge, he must use more strength, but WISDOM helps one succeed" (Ecc 10:10 ESV). Have you ever asked God to tell you something that you need to hear? Well, I did this morning, and I heard "Ecclesiastes 10" in my heart. I thought maybe I had said it to myself because it came so quickly. And to be honest, I have read that book recently and did not believe there was anything new I could get from it. That's because I had already gotten so many gems and profound truths from there. As I began reading, I was sure I had only heard my own voice until I hit verse ten (chapter ten, verse ten). To be sure, God used the ten twice to say that this is what I needed to hear. Working with a dull spirit saps my strength. I must be sharpened daily by the wisdom of God to do the work He has for me without exhausting myself. Spending time in God's word is my sharpening stone. If I don't start there, I become blunt and struggle to succeed.

20

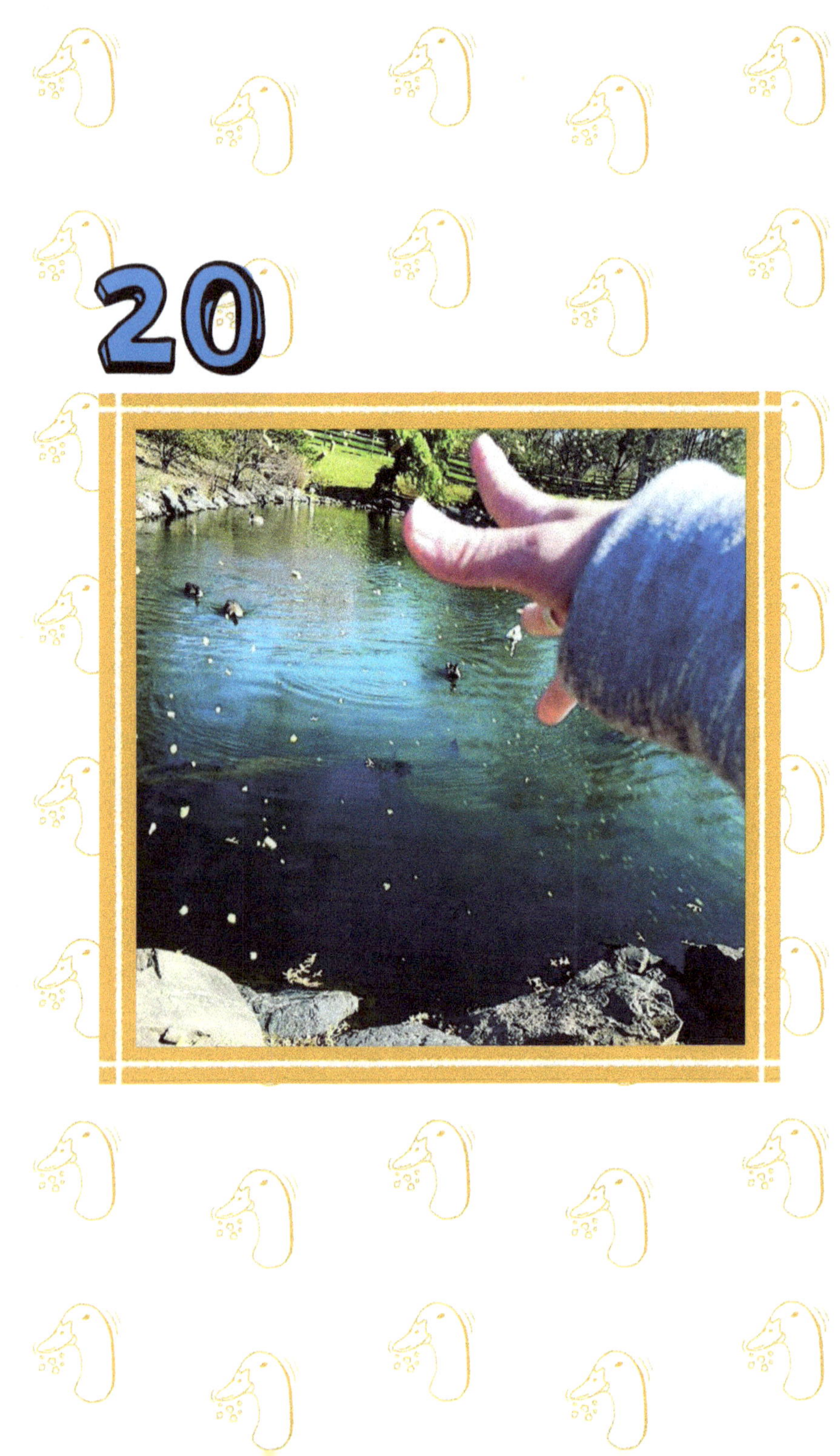

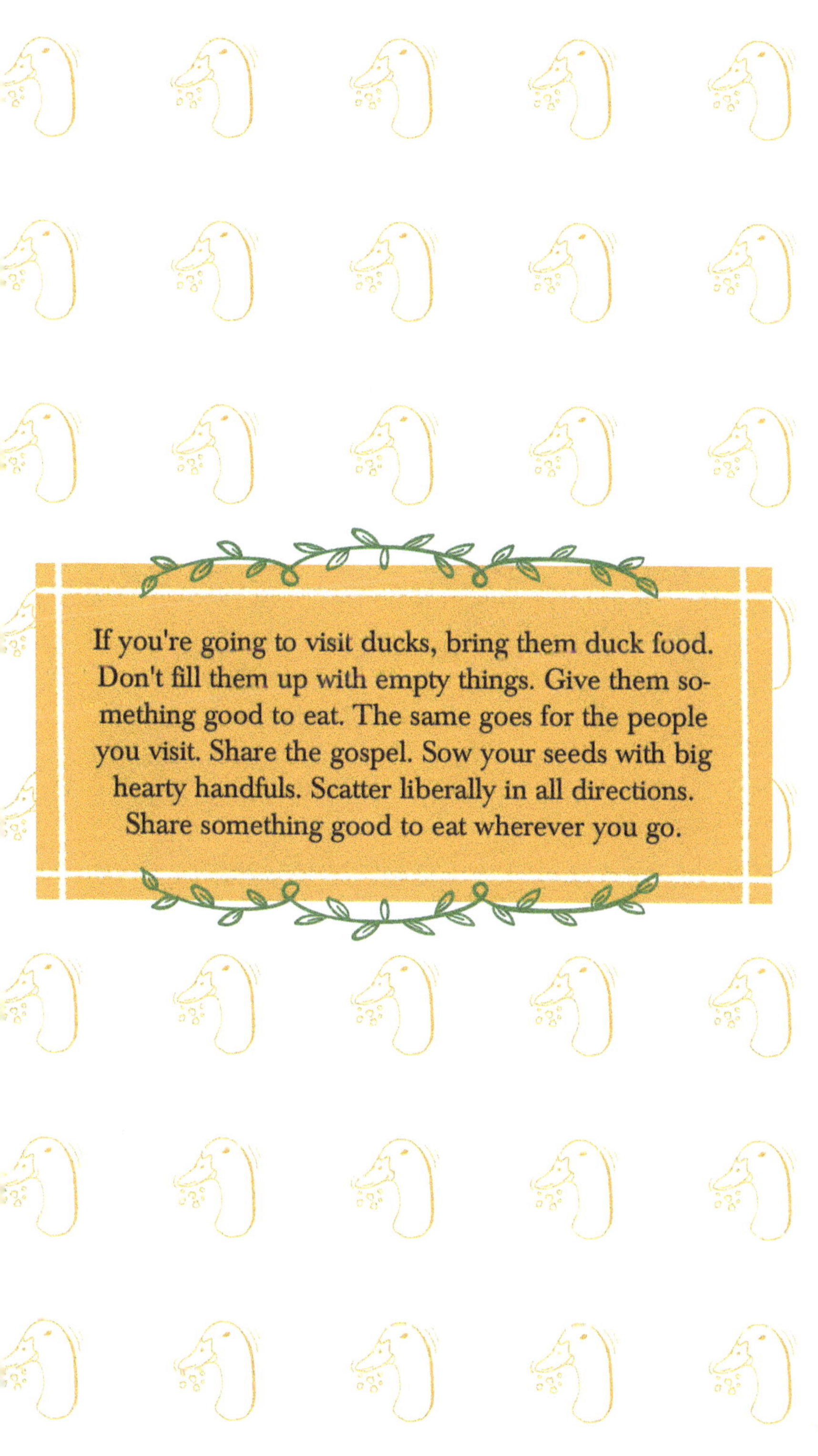

If you're going to visit ducks, bring them duck food. Don't fill them up with empty things. Give them something good to eat. The same goes for the people you visit. Share the gospel. Sow your seeds with big hearty handfuls. Scatter liberally in all directions. Share something good to eat wherever you go.

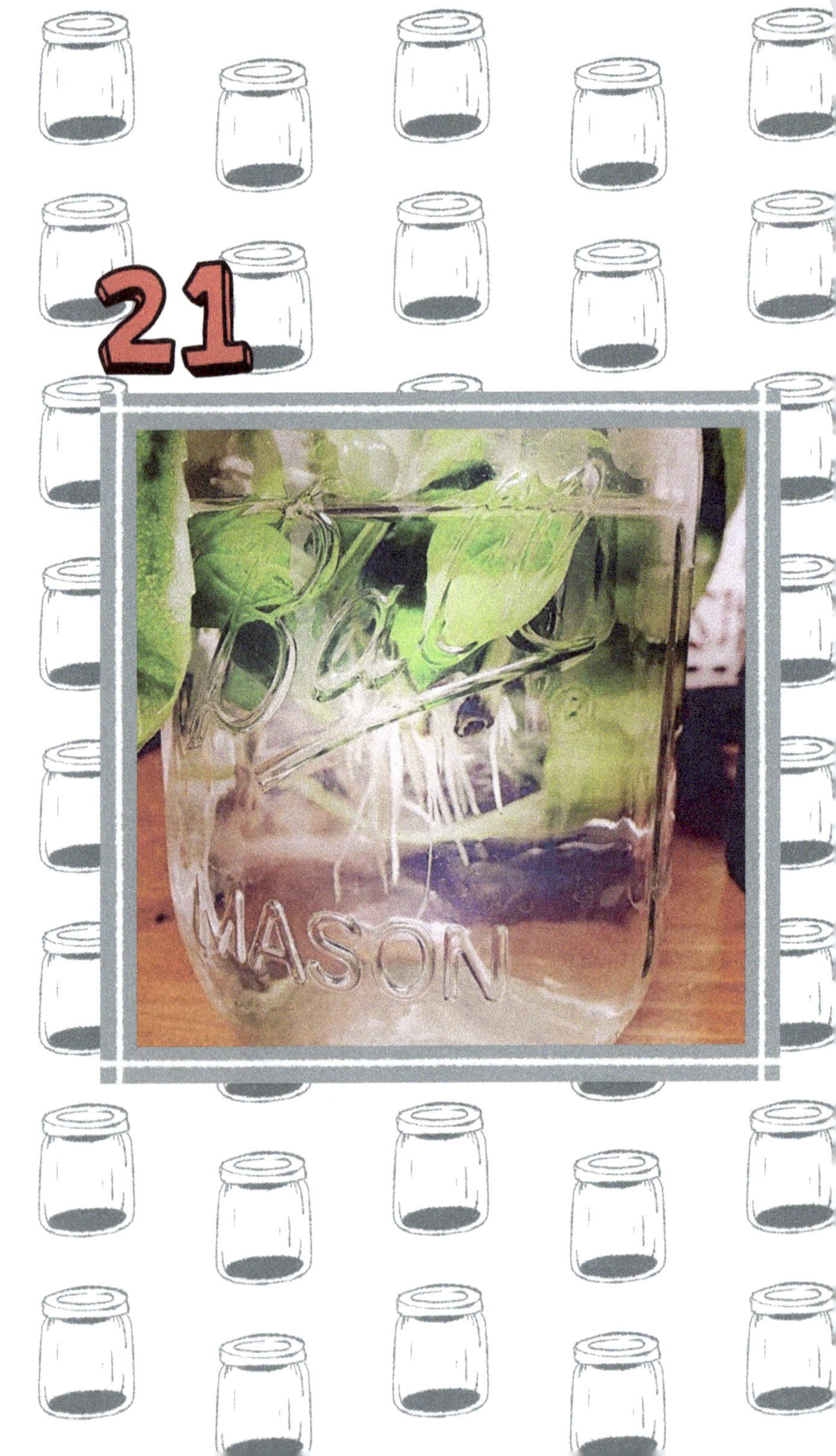
21
Ball
MASON

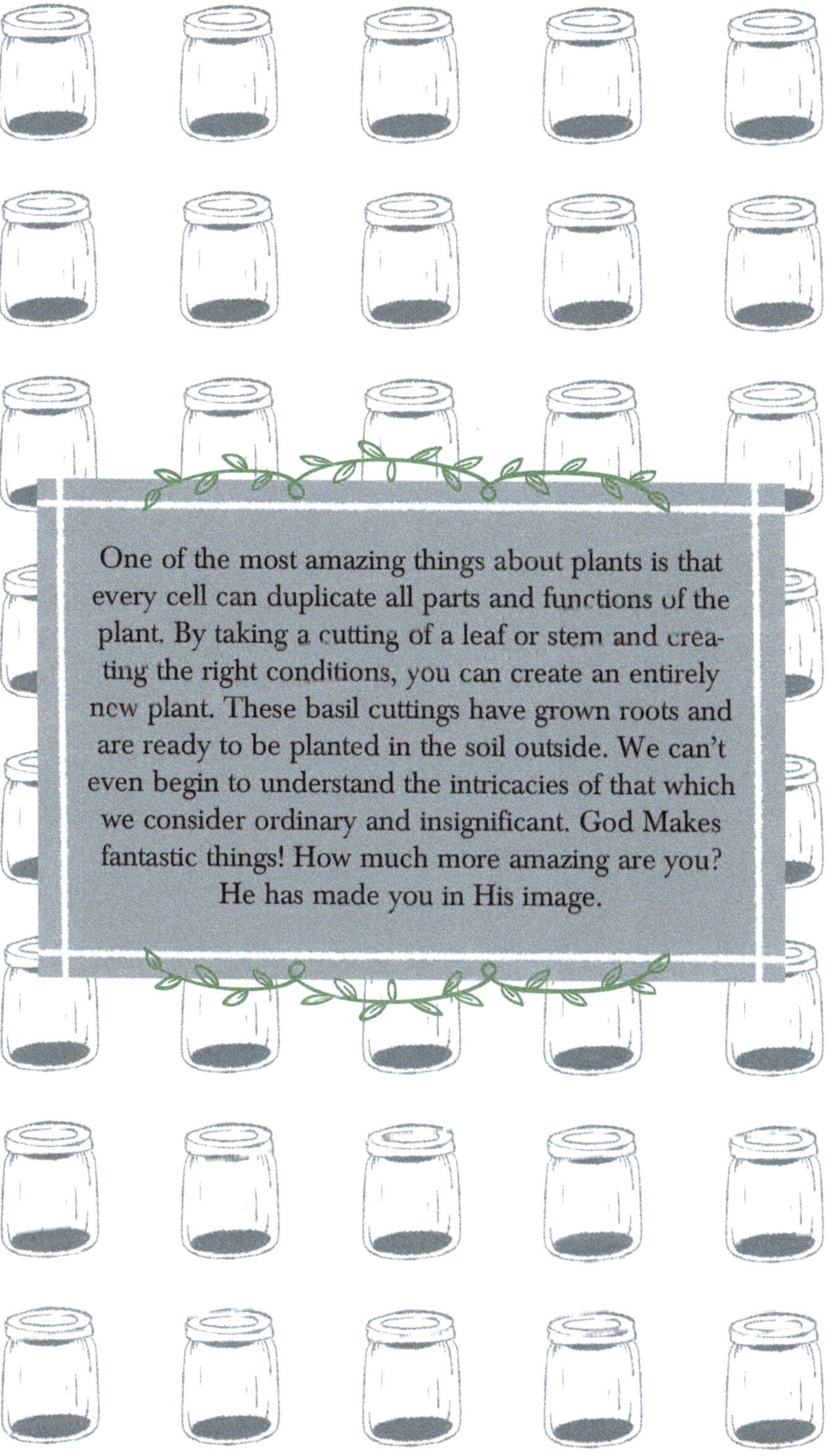

One of the most amazing things about plants is that every cell can duplicate all parts and functions of the plant. By taking a cutting of a leaf or stem and creating the right conditions, you can create an entirely new plant. These basil cuttings have grown roots and are ready to be planted in the soil outside. We can't even begin to understand the intricacies of that which we consider ordinary and insignificant. God Makes fantastic things! How much more amazing are you? He has made you in His image.

22

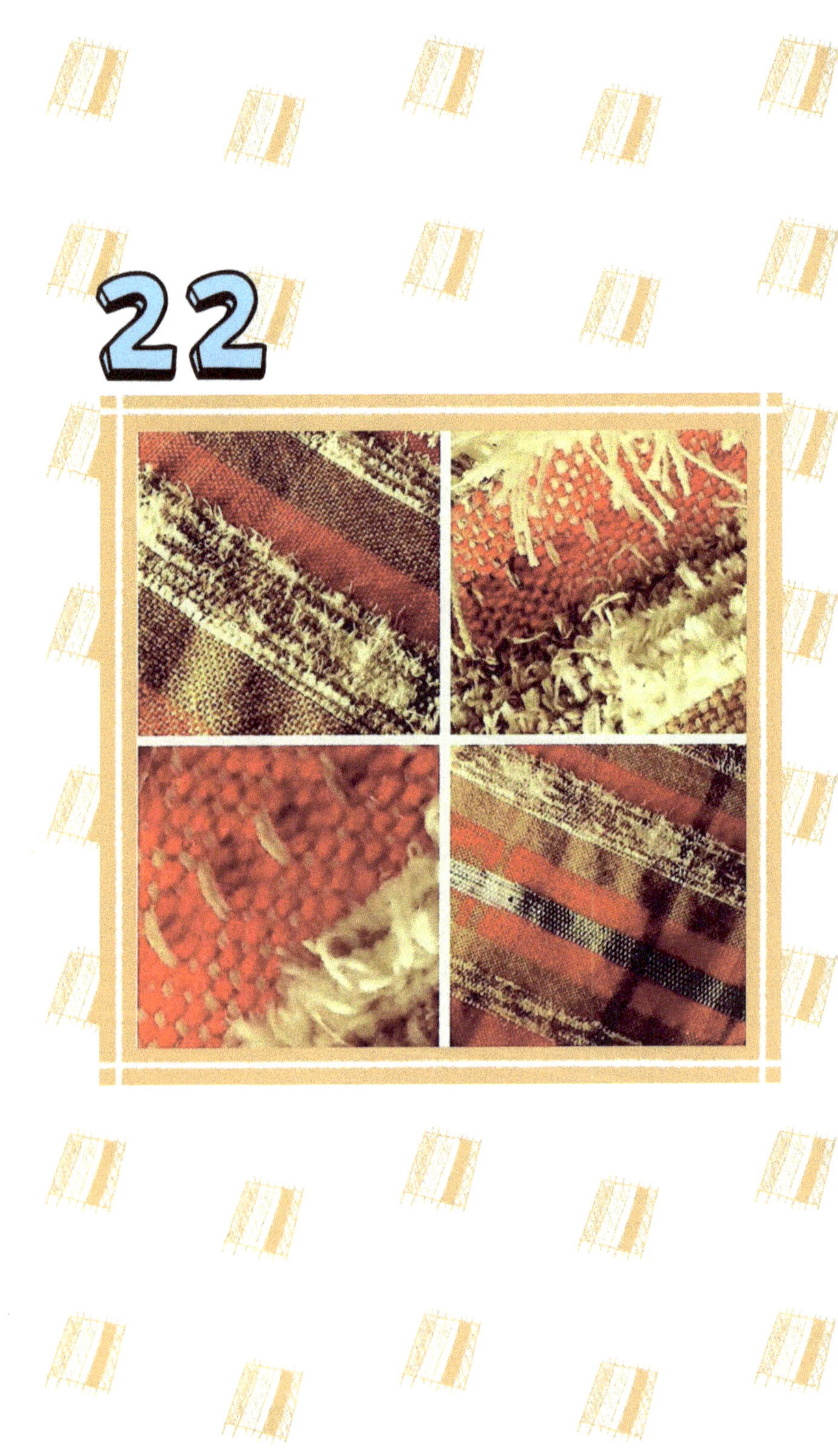

Our lives have mistakes woven into them. Like weaving this rug, only the one who is weaving knows what pattern they intended to create. The observer can only see what is in front of them. When you make a mistake or take a wrong turn, but learn from it, it can be a beautiful thing. When you look at your life in its entirety, that place can turn out to be the most beautiful part! (I wove this rug with a friend who was kind enough to teach me and then let me try it on my own). Only I know where the mistakes are, but they remind me of what I learned to do correctly, not of what I did wrong.

23

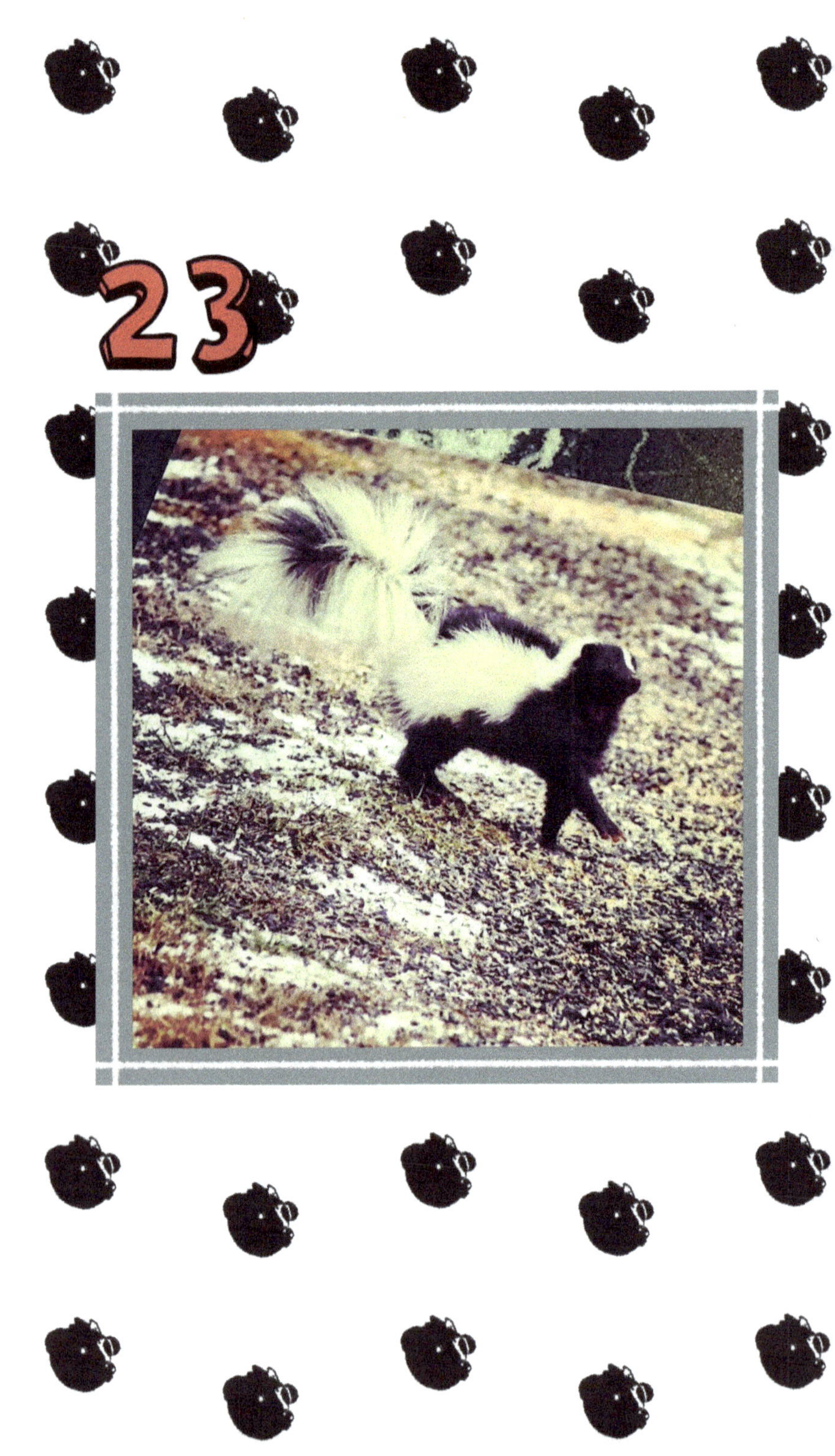

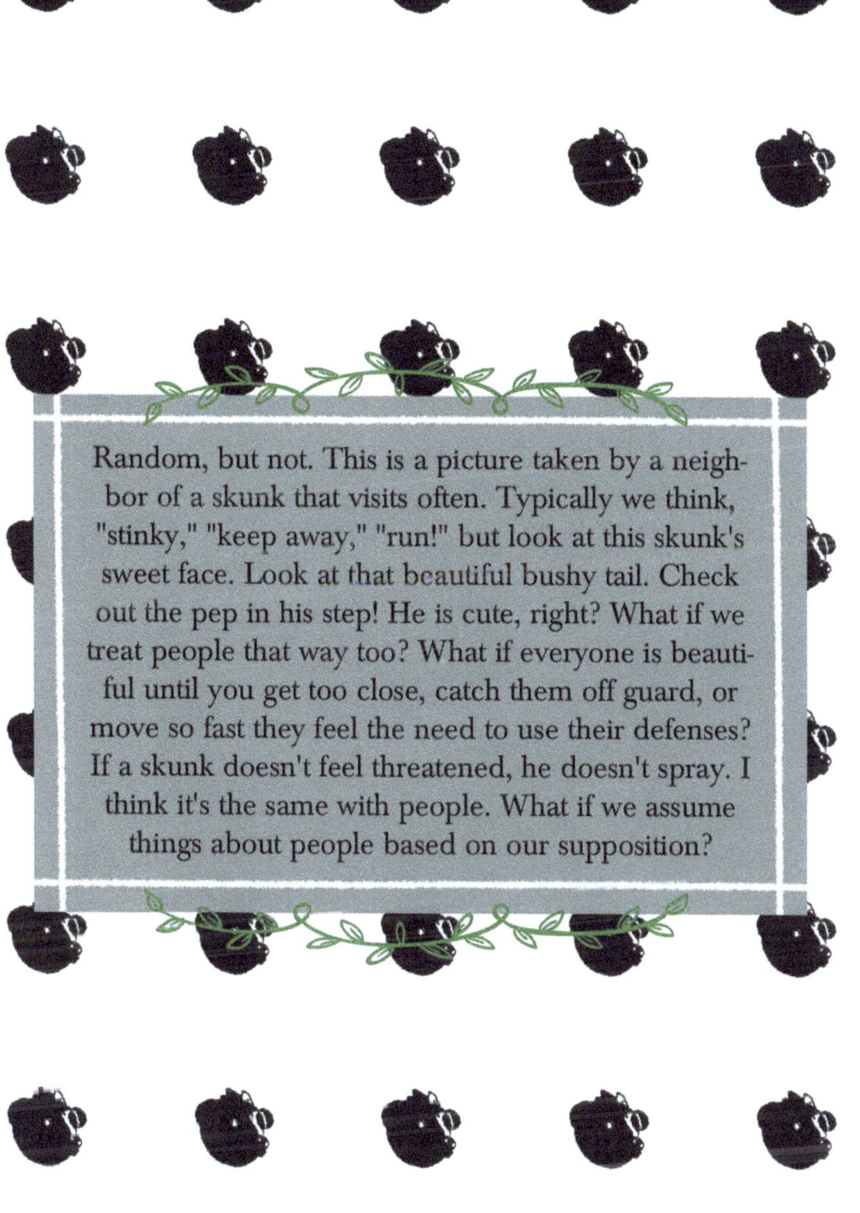

Random, but not. This is a picture taken by a neighbor of a skunk that visits often. Typically we think, "stinky," "keep away," "run!" but look at this skunk's sweet face. Look at that beautiful bushy tail. Check out the pep in his step! He is cute, right? What if we treat people that way too? What if everyone is beautiful until you get too close, catch them off guard, or move so fast they feel the need to use their defenses? If a skunk doesn't feel threatened, he doesn't spray. I think it's the same with people. What if we assume things about people based on our supposition?

24

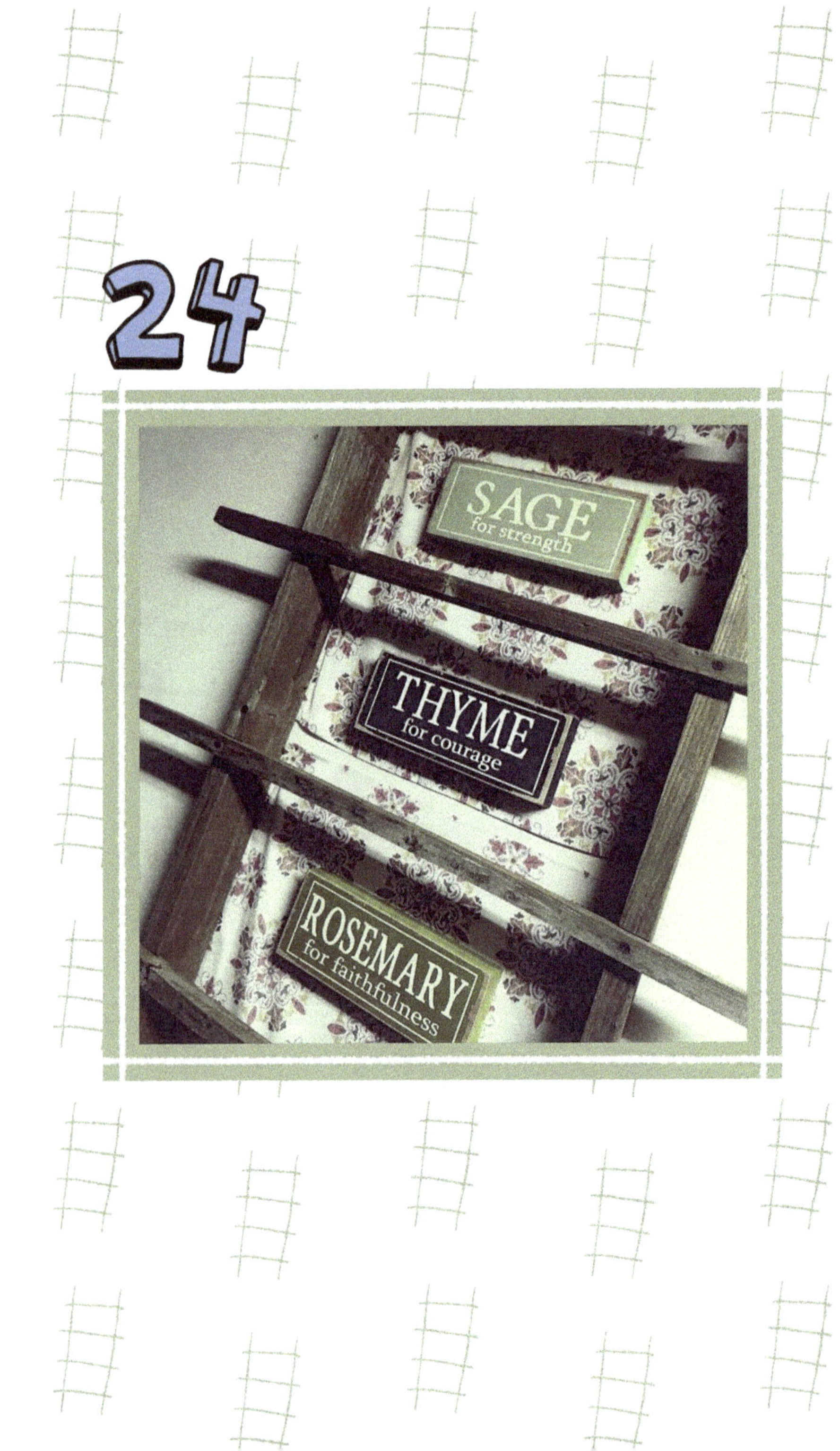

SAGE
for strength
THYME
for courage
ROSEMARY
for faithfulness

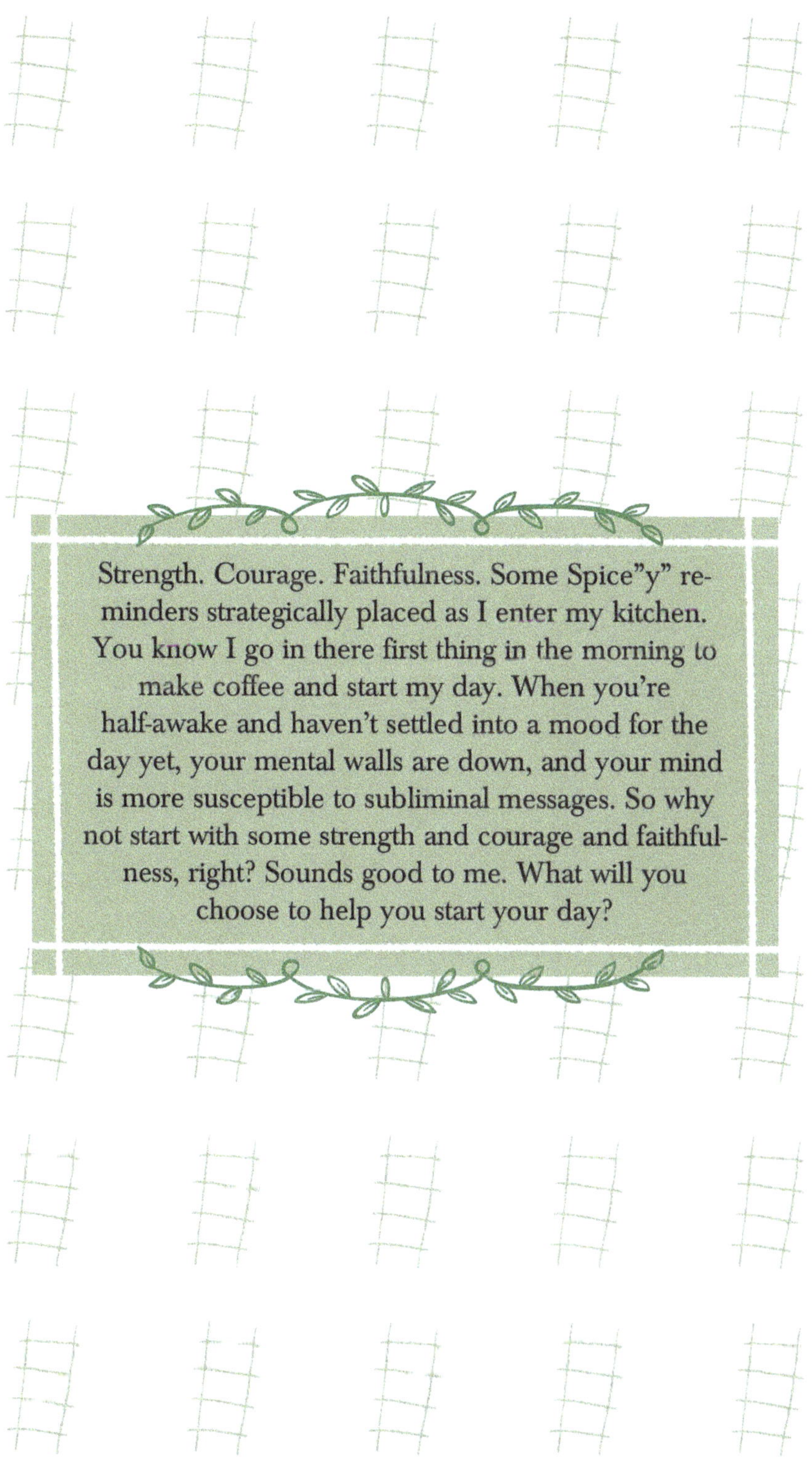

Strength. Courage. Faithfulness. Some Spice"y" reminders strategically placed as I enter my kitchen.
You know I go in there first thing in the morning to
make coffee and start my day. When you're
half-awake and haven't settled into a mood for the
day yet, your mental walls are down, and your mind
is more susceptible to subliminal messages. So why
not start with some strength and courage and faithfulness, right? Sounds good to me. What will you
choose to help you start your day?

25

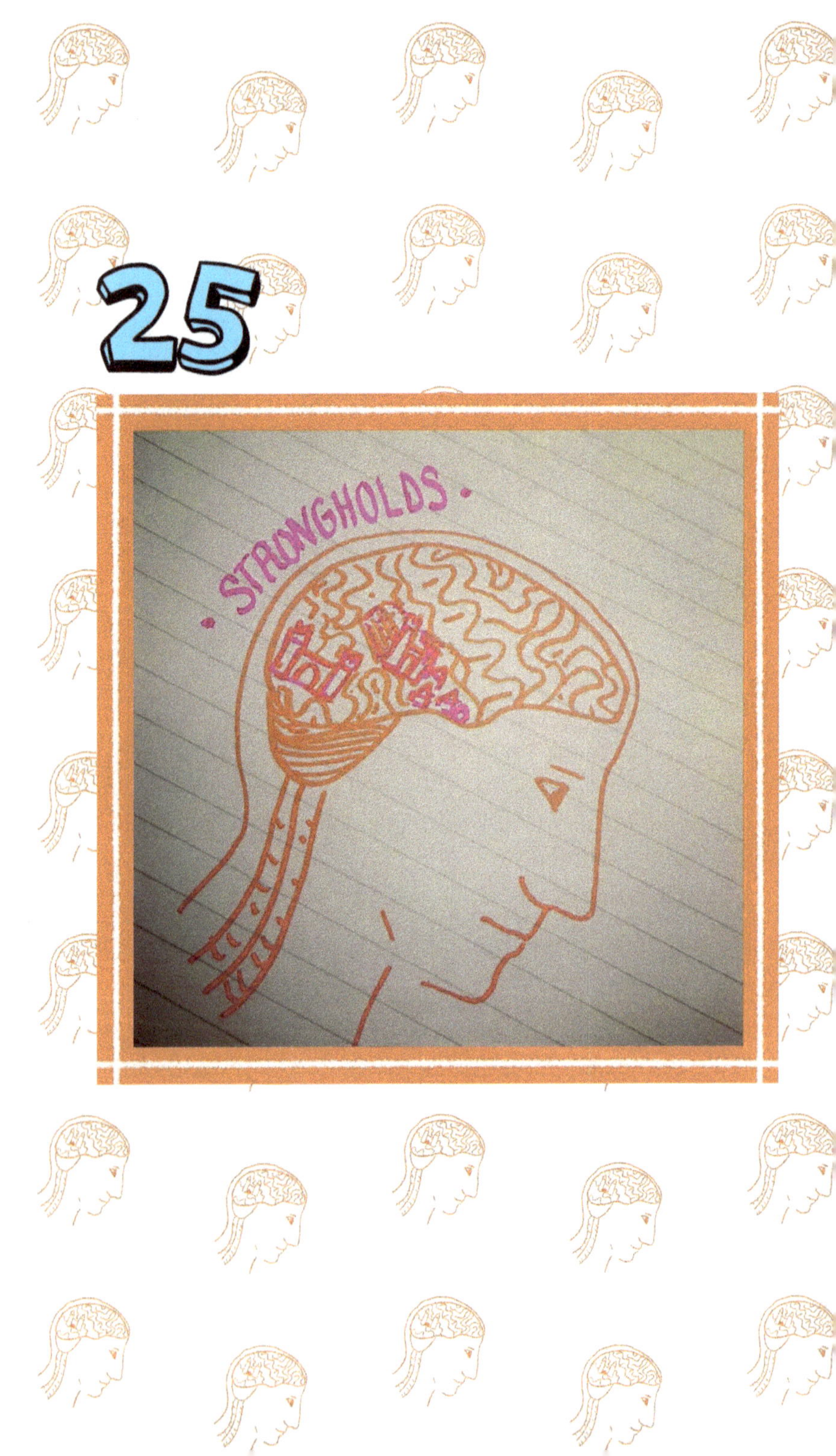

Strongholds in your mind, a weighty subject I was discussing with my son, and what he said blew me away! We decided that strongholds were little villages and cities, places of resistance in your mind that led to rebellion with God in your heart. My son then said that when he realized that he was defending his strongholds himself, that he had built them and not some foreign enemy, that he had defended them, my son said that he (that we) could at any time let them fall and be conquered by Christ as we allow Him access. Well, who says you can't learn from your kids? I set out to draw a few pictures in my journal and jot down some reality from that discussion today so as not to convince myself otherwise next time I try to justify my rebellions before God. Do not be deceived by self-sabotage.

26

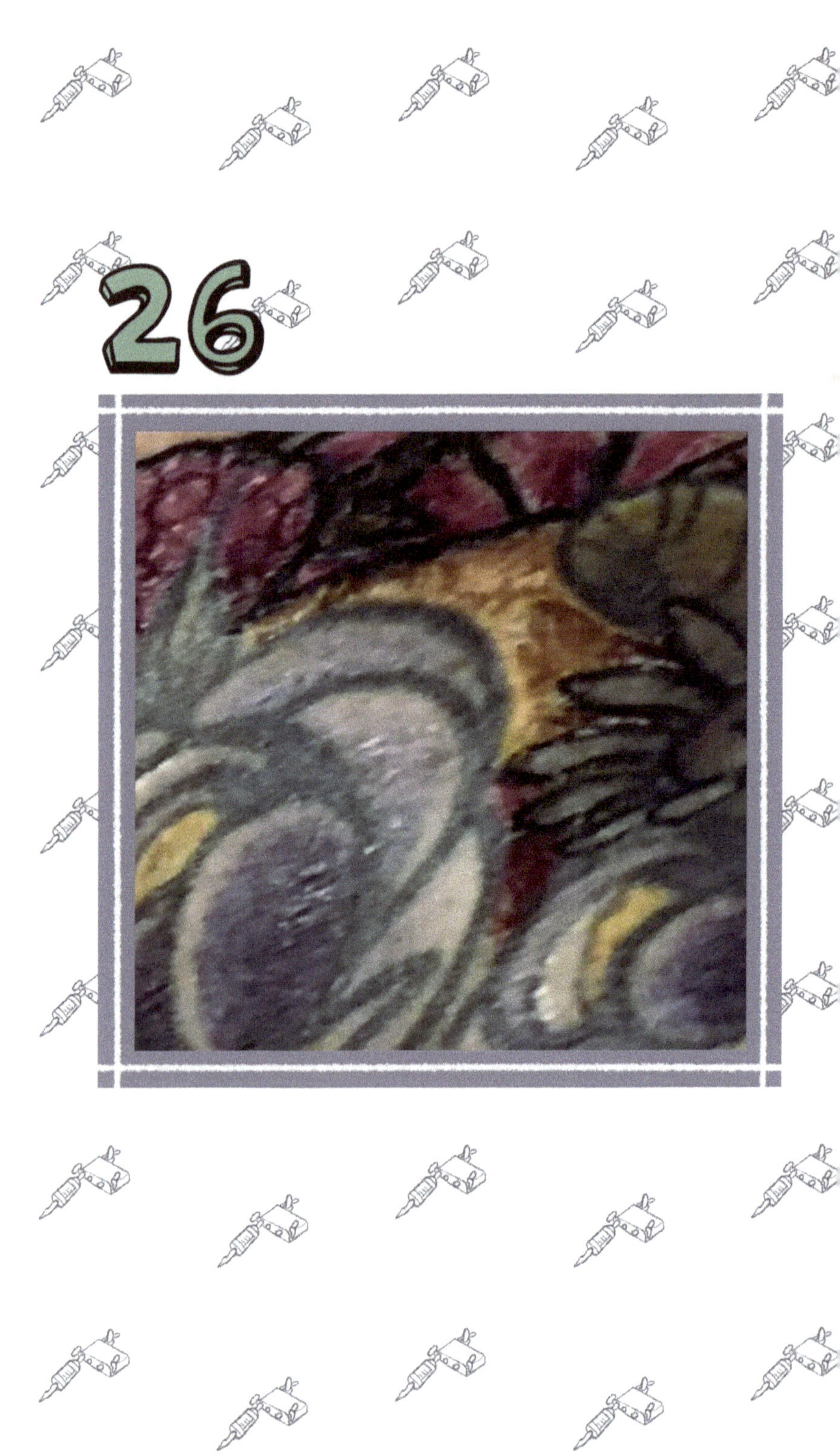

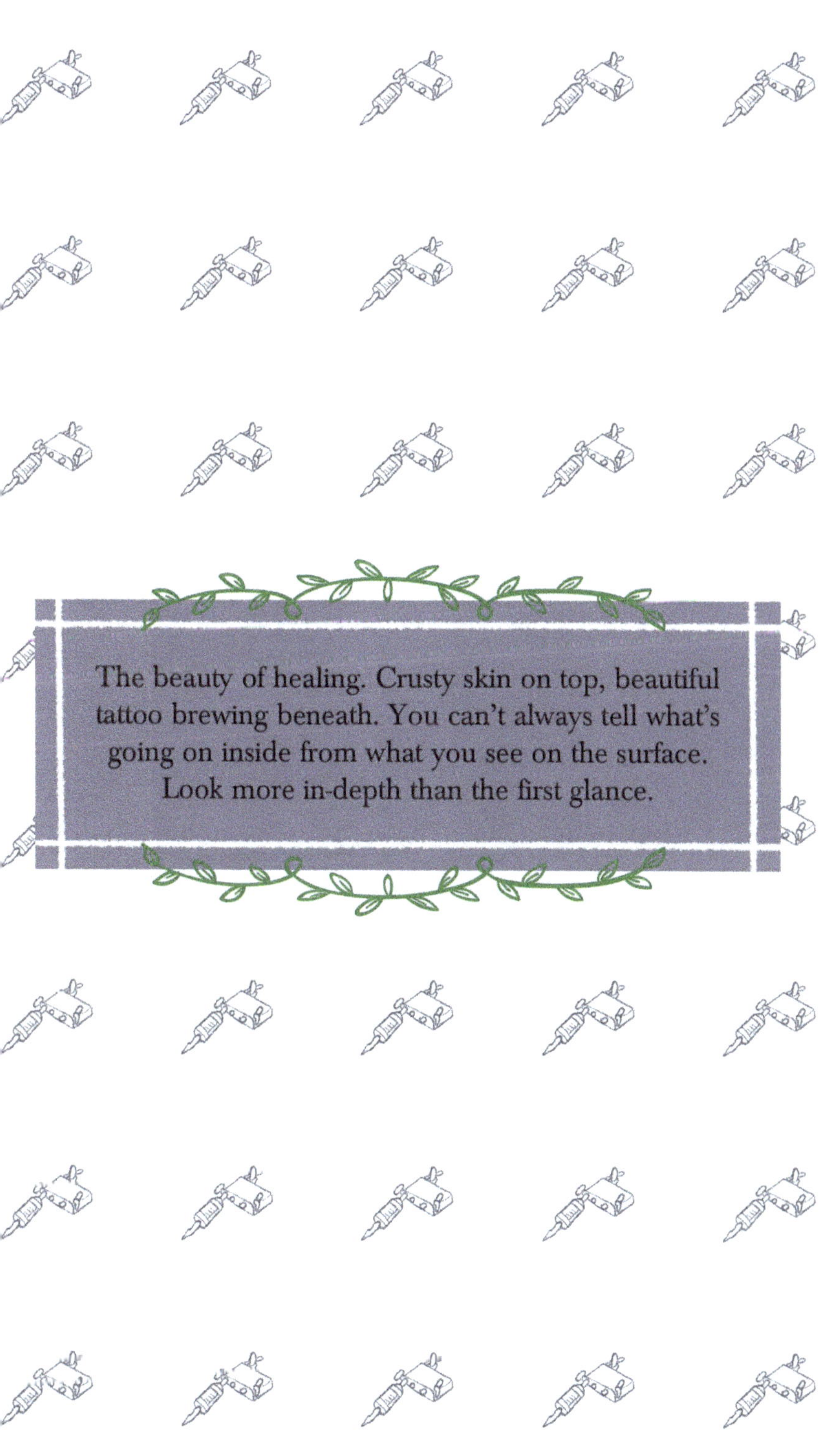

The beauty of healing. Crusty skin on top, beautiful tattoo brewing beneath. You can't always tell what's going on inside from what you see on the surface. Look more in-depth than the first glance.

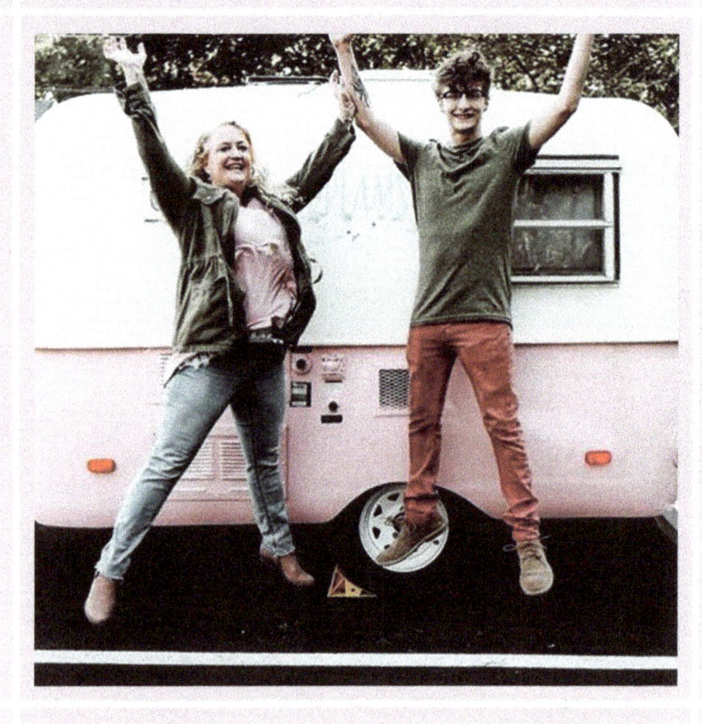

27

The plans God has for your life don't feel like work. Don't get me wrong, they take diligence, commitment, and effort, but they have been handcrafted just for you. If you wait for God's instruction and His timing, you will find that you get to use every bit of yourself, that He made you just right for the task He has given you. And as you work, instead of becoming tired, you come alive. It's so much fun to step into a plan of God. It's incredible to get to do what He made you for, and in my case, I get to do it with one of my favorite people. Don't just know what you're supposed to do, go and do it!

28

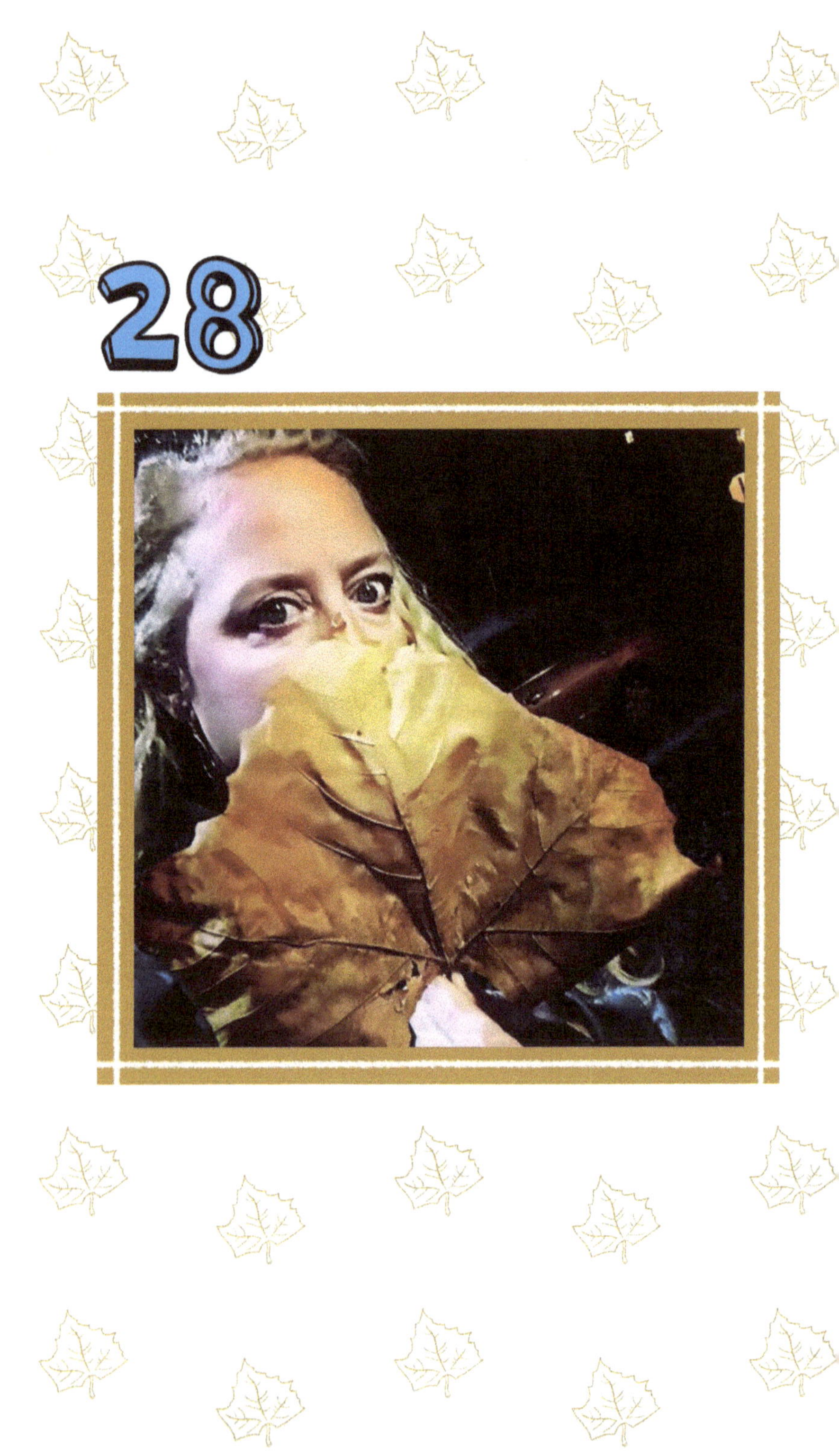

This Sycamore leaf was in the grass. It looked so ridiculously large next to the other leaves (we don't have any Sycamore trees near here). It must have come to me on the wind. I wonder how some things come into our lives, some things that don't seem like the others, things that don't seem to belong. I had a person like that once. They just showed up in my "yard." It turns out, they had an agenda, and I, being sweet and trusting, just picked them up and brought them in and held them close. Sometimes we need to check in with our surroundings and ask a few questions. It's hard being kind. People see kindness as a weakness, but it is the strongest of strengths to stay kind when the world can be so cruel. The Bible says to be "Wise as a serpent and as harmless as a dove." It says that we are, "Sent out as sheep among wolves" in the book of Mathew, chapter ten. The world can be hostile to the things of God, and we have an enemy of our souls. So stay kind but be wise. Not everyone belongs in your yard

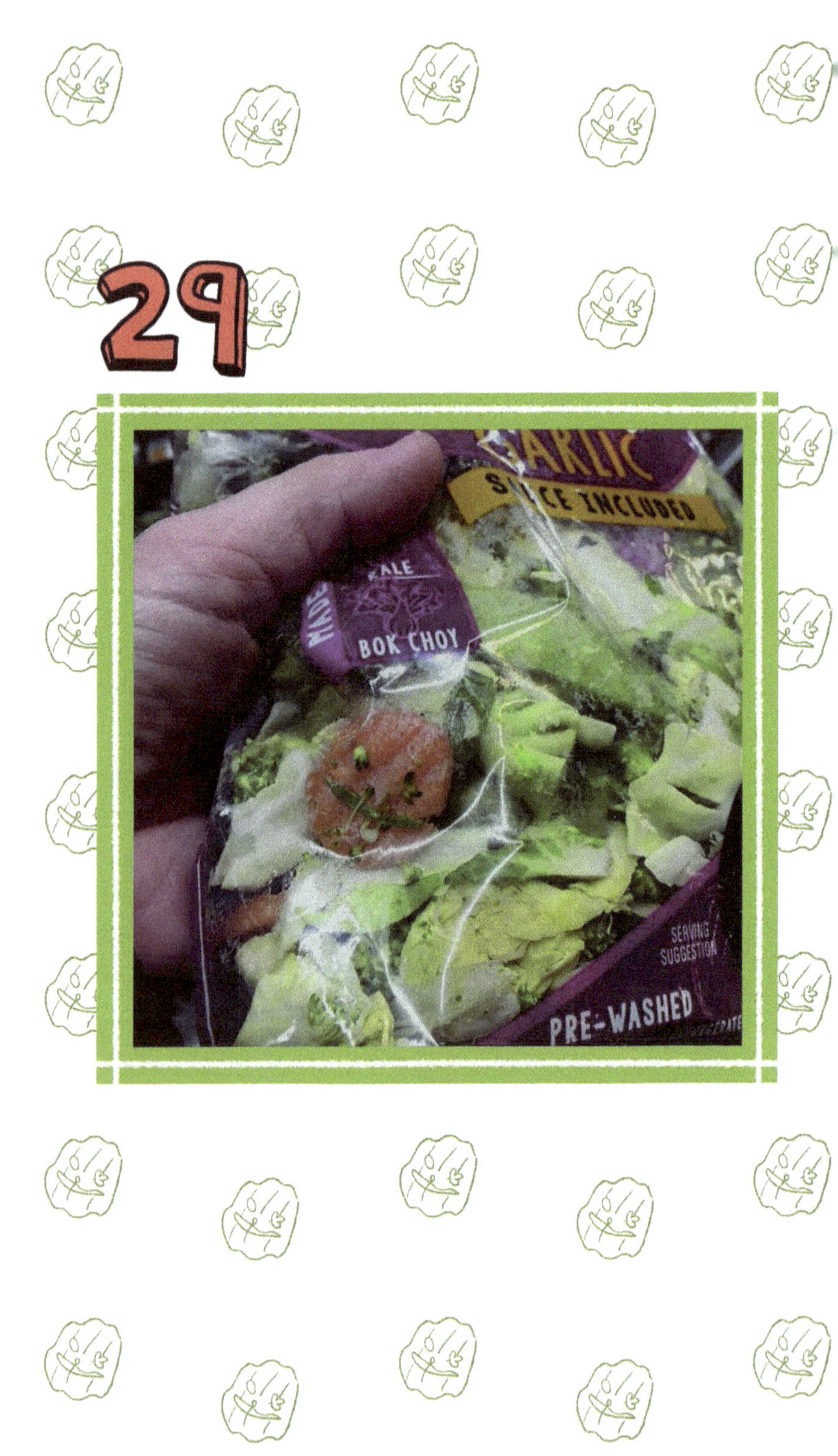
GARLIC
SAUCE INCLUDED
KALE
MADE
BOK CHOY
SERVING
SUGGESTION
PRE-WASHED

29

When I Looked down, my stir fry mix was smiling up at me. As soon as I saw that goofy carrot smiling at me, I found myself smiling too. How can something so silly and little make a difference? I quickly took a picture with my phone and then put the bag into my shopping cart, and as soon as I did, the contents shifted, and my funny little friend immediately disappeared. I guess my point is this: I could have missed it. So often we are moving so fast, not interacting with our surroundings. We are on our phones or rushing to get to the next moment or filled with thoughts from the moments that came before, and we miss the present, the "presents" which God has placed there just for us. We don't see the messages and the words He has for us. To be honest I needed to laugh at that moment, to feel the wonder of a child discovering a little friend. Children see with their hearts and they believe anything can happen. God said His name is "I AM" when Moses asked Him. Did you ever think that part of why He is called that is that life, real LIFE is what is happening right now? Not yesterday or tomorrow but now. So look around and enjoy your "right now "and know that God is with you in it.

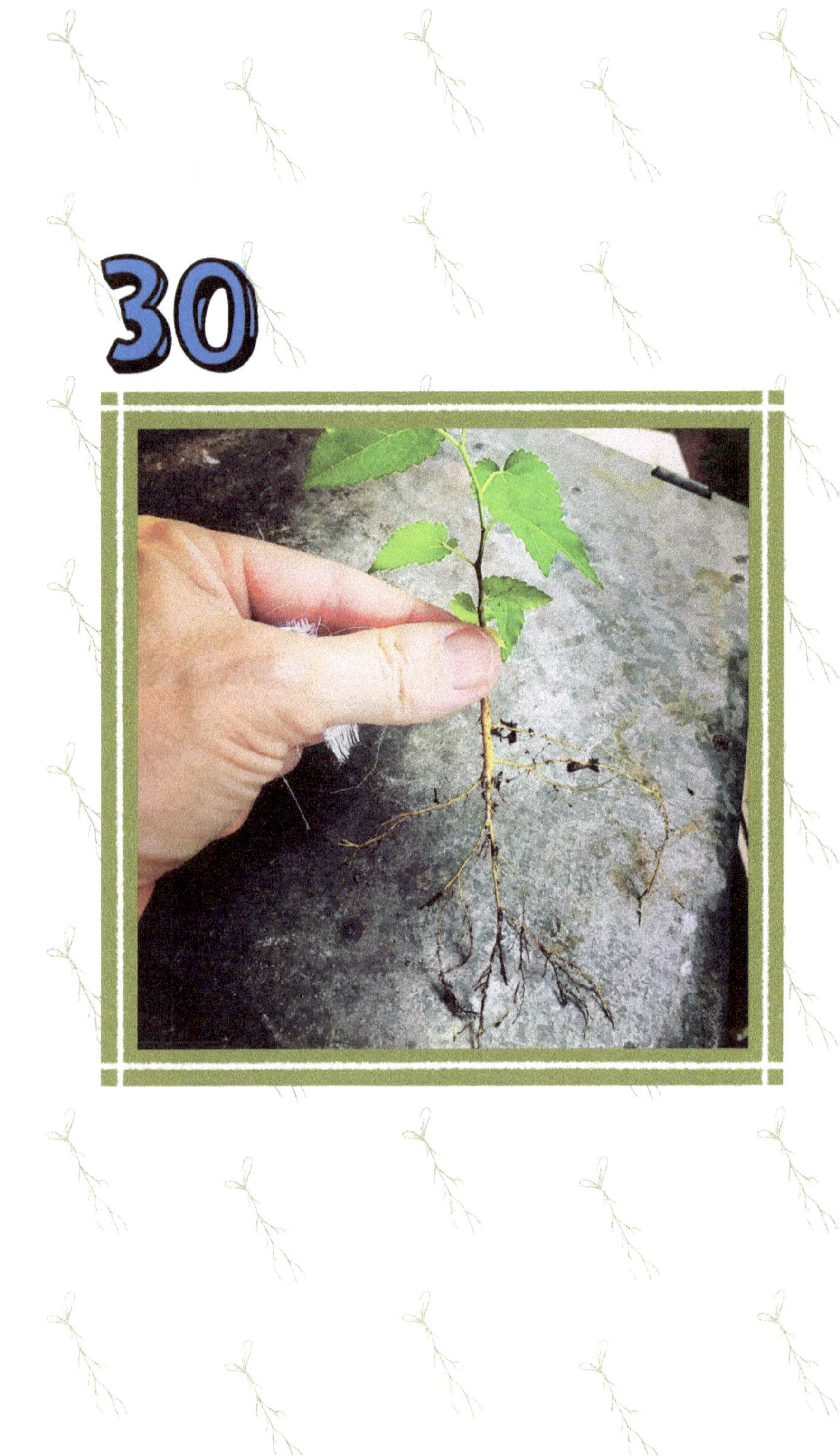

30

This little guy sprang up overnight. It was growing between the deck boards at the outer edge of the balcony past the railing. Look how big the roots are! It made me think. We see tiny weeds growing in our lives and think, "Ah I'll get around to it, I can always pluck that out when I have time." These roots are big enough to start sending up new plants. Before you know it, you can have a patch and then a crop. At the first sign of something springing up in your heart that you didn't intentionally plant, make sure it's not something you should pluck out while you still can. You can't just look at what's going on on the surface. A lot is going on deep within.

31

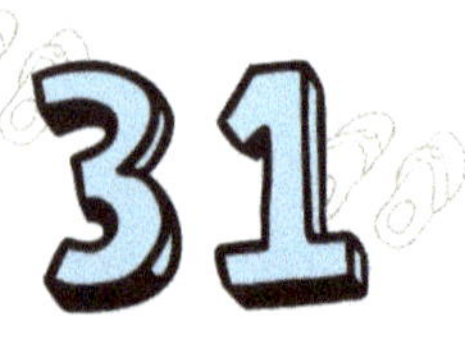

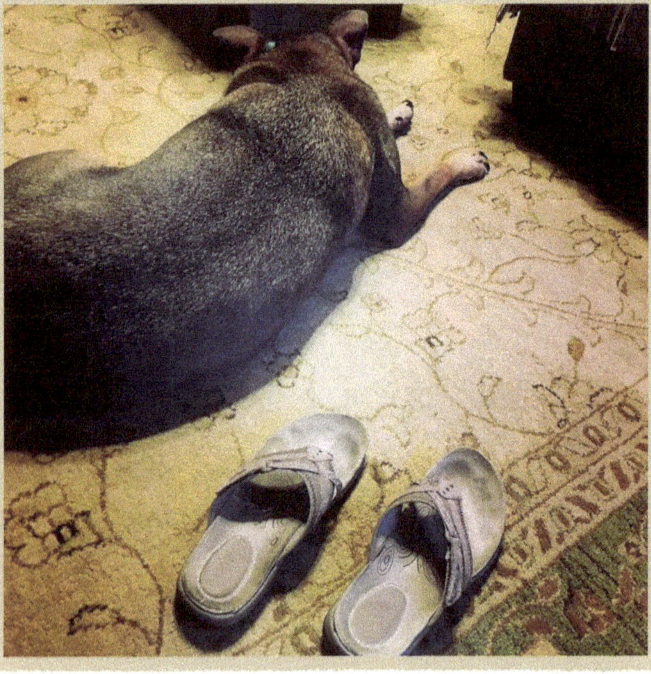

This morning's worship resulted in a poem. Shoes off, heart open, waiting to receive. Eyes closed, heart posed to encounter, to believe. Silent, settled, still before the Lord. Expectant, humbled, kneeling on the floor. Arms raised, lips praise the One who's called me home. His kindness and His love have made me His own. The King of everything and the daughter He's brought home. They finally sit together, no longer alone.

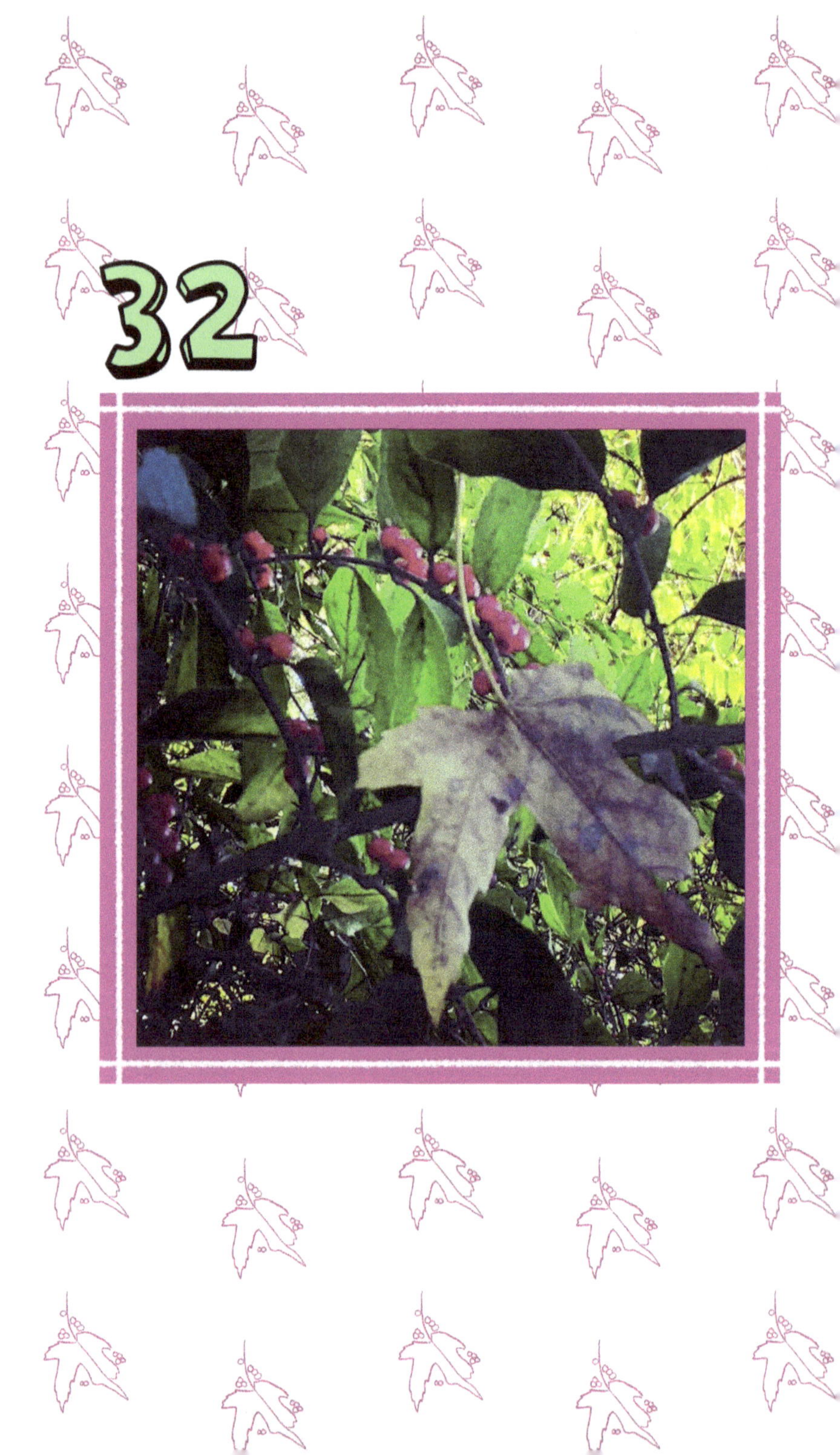

32

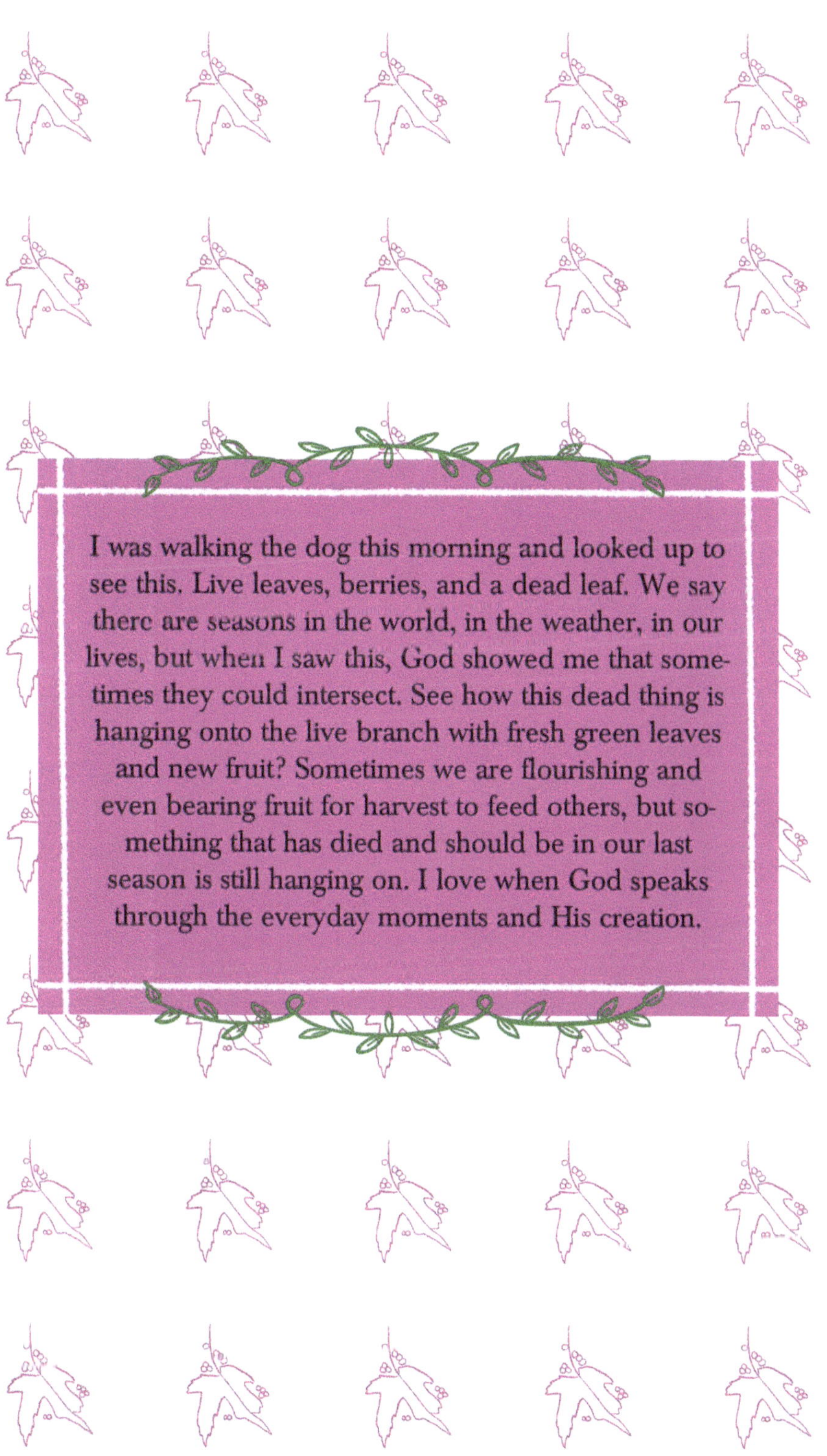

I was walking the dog this morning and looked up to see this. Live leaves, berries, and a dead leaf. We say there are seasons in the world, in the weather, in our lives, but when I saw this, God showed me that sometimes they could intersect. See how this dead thing is hanging onto the live branch with fresh green leaves and new fruit? Sometimes we are flourishing and even bearing fruit for harvest to feed others, but something that has died and should be in our last season is still hanging on. I love when God speaks through the everyday moments and His creation.

33

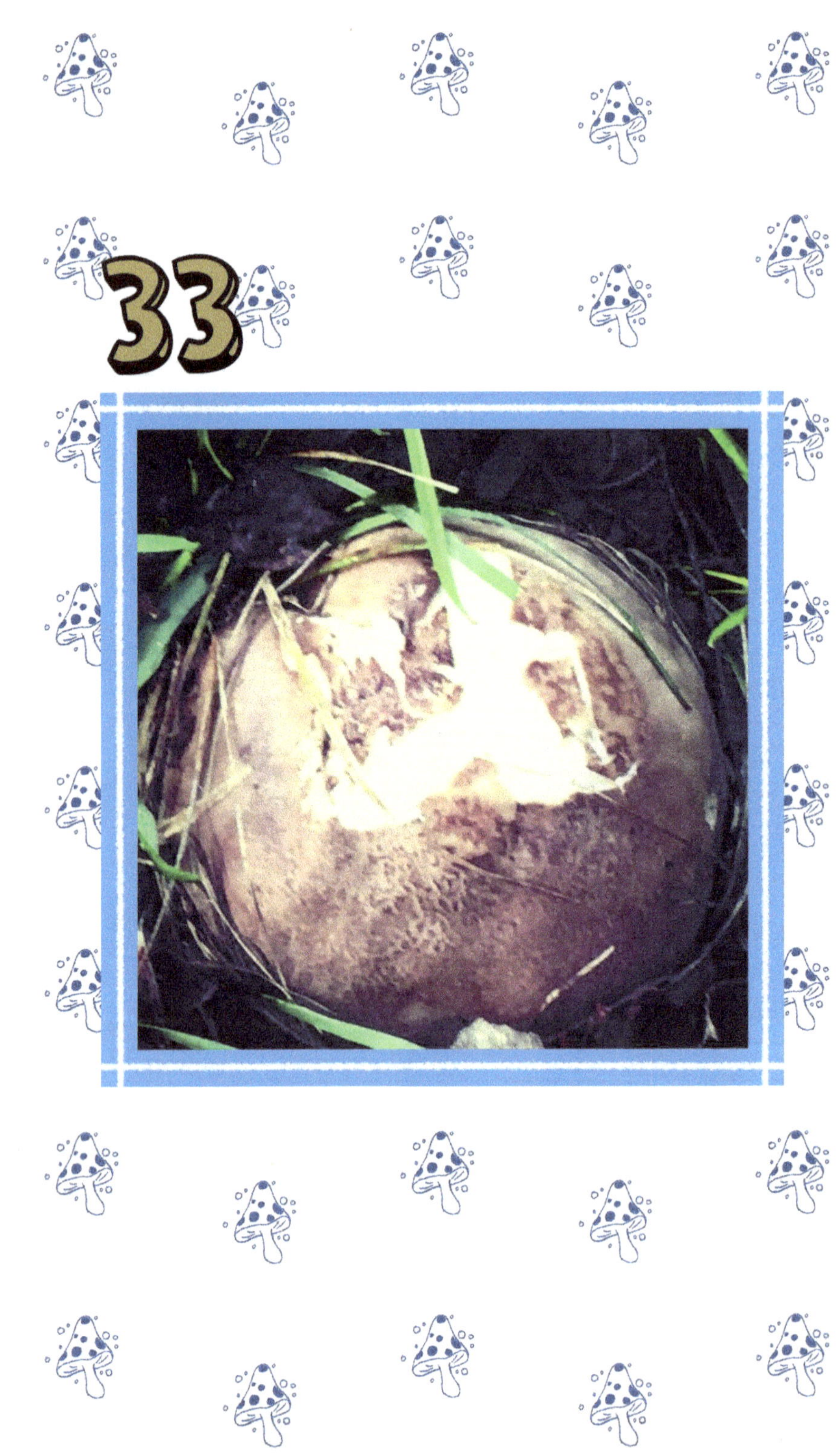

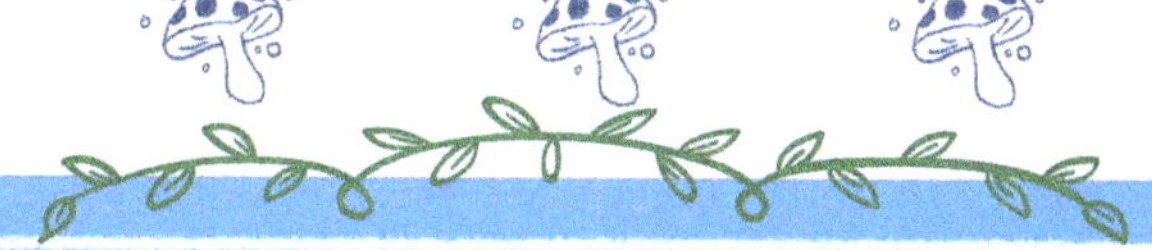

This gigantic mushroom (it was the size of a softball) was hidden under all of the leaves. I stepped on it and almost fell. It's just doing its thing growing in the darkness and under cover of the debris of broken down and dying leaves. As I caught myself, I thought, "Wow I didn't even know that was there." How did I miss something that big? And immediately God showed me that there are things under the surface, covered over by debris left from everything, not of His kingdom. The areas we haven't cleared out yet from our life before accepting Him that still scatter the floor of our hearts. They pile up in the dark, and if you don't rake them up and sift through what's there, in the darkness, in that quiet atmosphere of neglect, new things will grow. And so another everyday moment morning lesson from God. I have some raking to do! How about you?

34

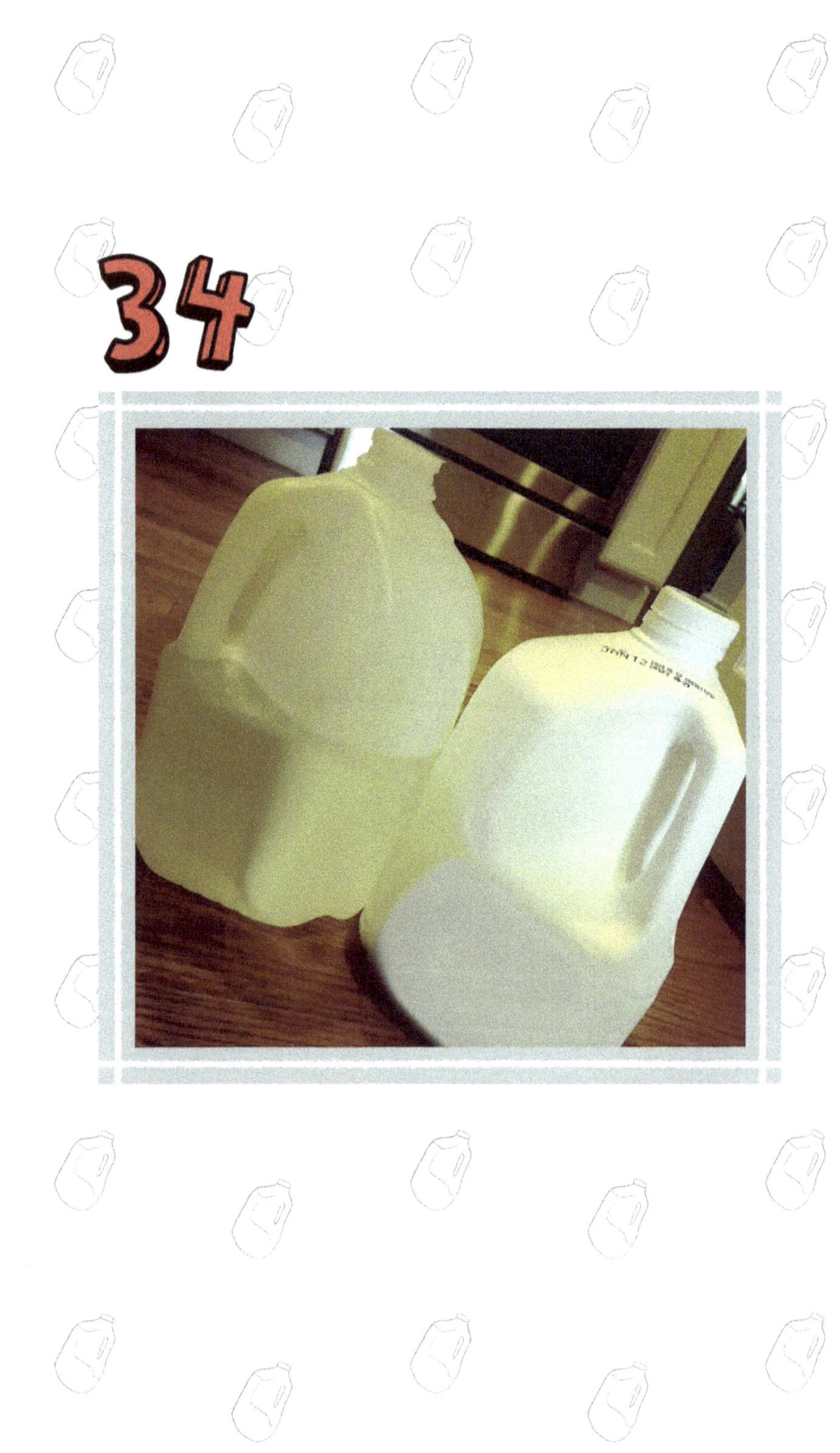

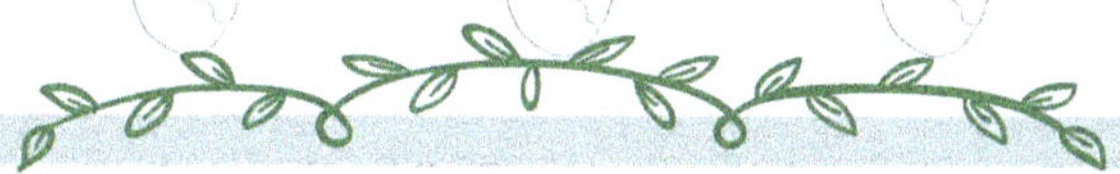

These two look a lot alike on the outside. And if you didn't look when pulling one out of the fridge, they feel quite the same as well. That's what I did this morning. The water was in the milk's usual spot. I pulled it out and began to pour it without looking at the label. Watery cereal anyone? Of course, it made me think, "Just because something is similar to something else doesn't mean that what's inside is the same." I've noticed that the enemy likes to make something look so much like the truth, so much like what he is impersonating, that if someone doesn't check twice, they will think they have one thing when what they have is something entirely different. For this reason, my friends we need to test all things by the word of God. It may look good, even feel good, but if it isn't one hundred percent what we think it is, what's inside will infiltrate our hearts. Heavy theology from such a little mix-up, I know, but welcome to my world.

35

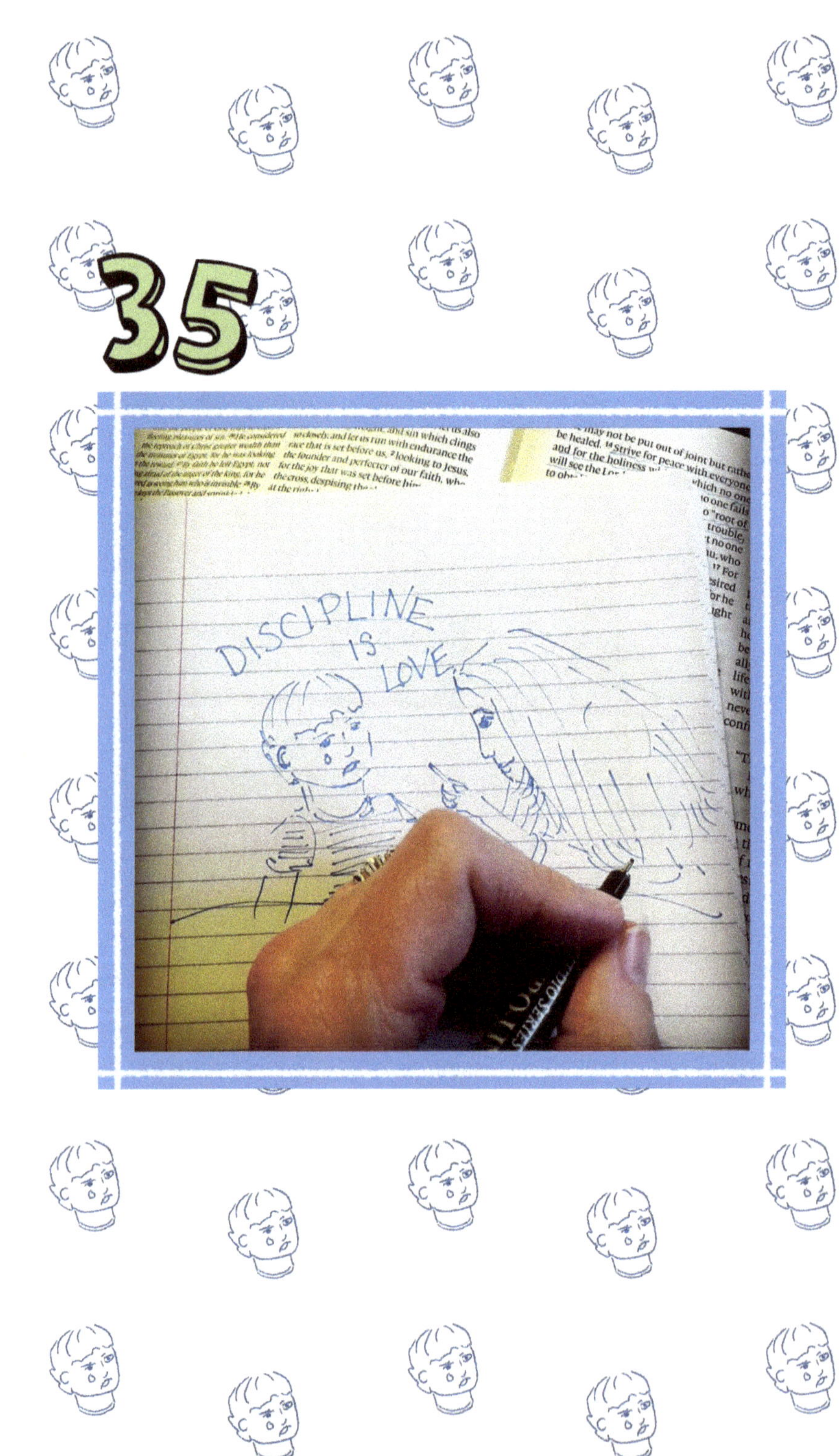

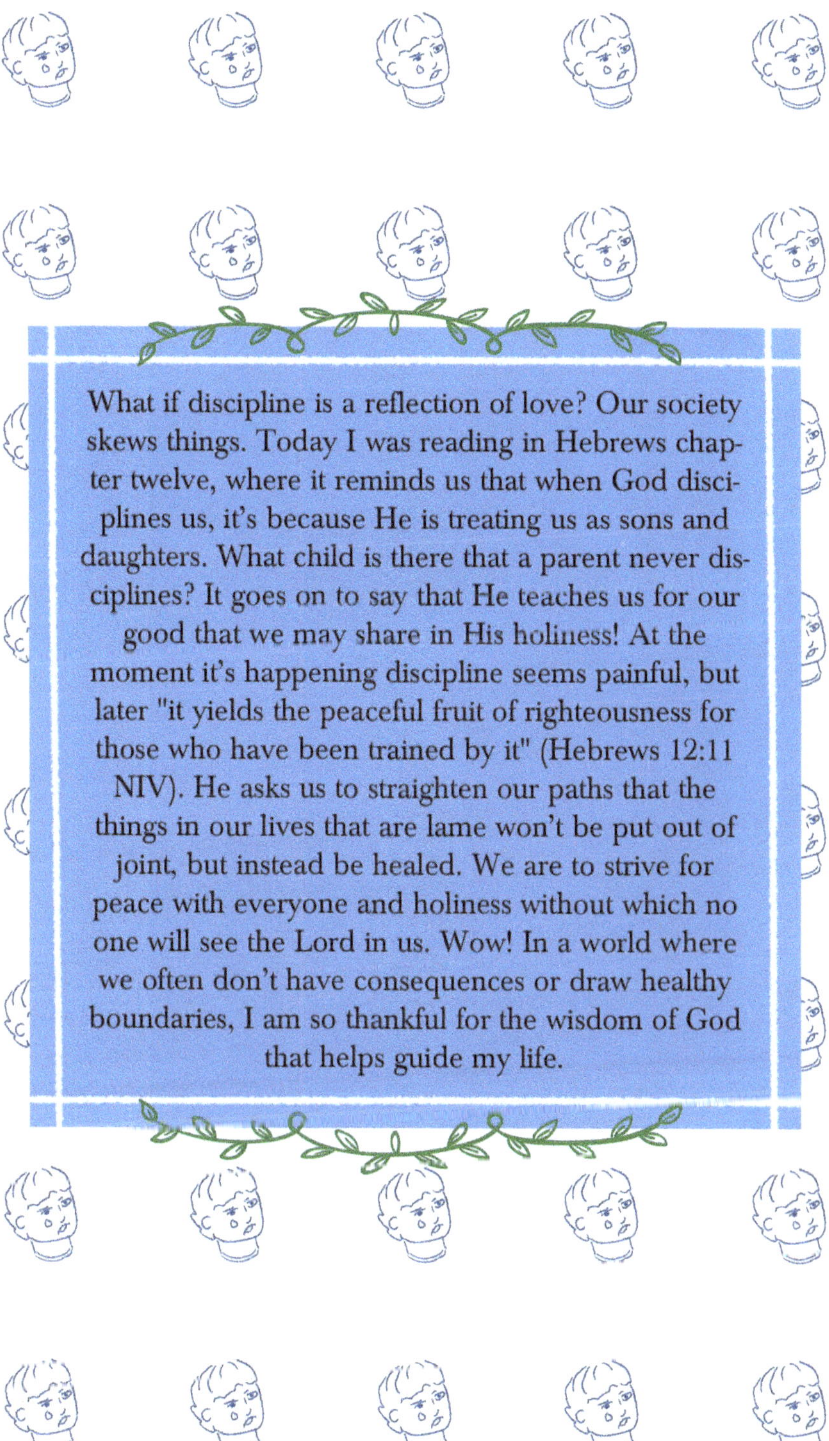

What if discipline is a reflection of love? Our society skews things. Today I was reading in Hebrews chapter twelve, where it reminds us that when God disciplines us, it's because He is treating us as sons and daughters. What child is there that a parent never disciplines? It goes on to say that He teaches us for our good that we may share in His holiness! At the moment it's happening discipline seems painful, but later "it yields the peaceful fruit of righteousness for those who have been trained by it" (Hebrews 12:11 NIV). He asks us to straighten our paths that the things in our lives that are lame won't be put out of joint, but instead be healed. We are to strive for peace with everyone and holiness without which no one will see the Lord in us. Wow! In a world where we often don't have consequences or draw healthy boundaries, I am so thankful for the wisdom of God that helps guide my life.

36

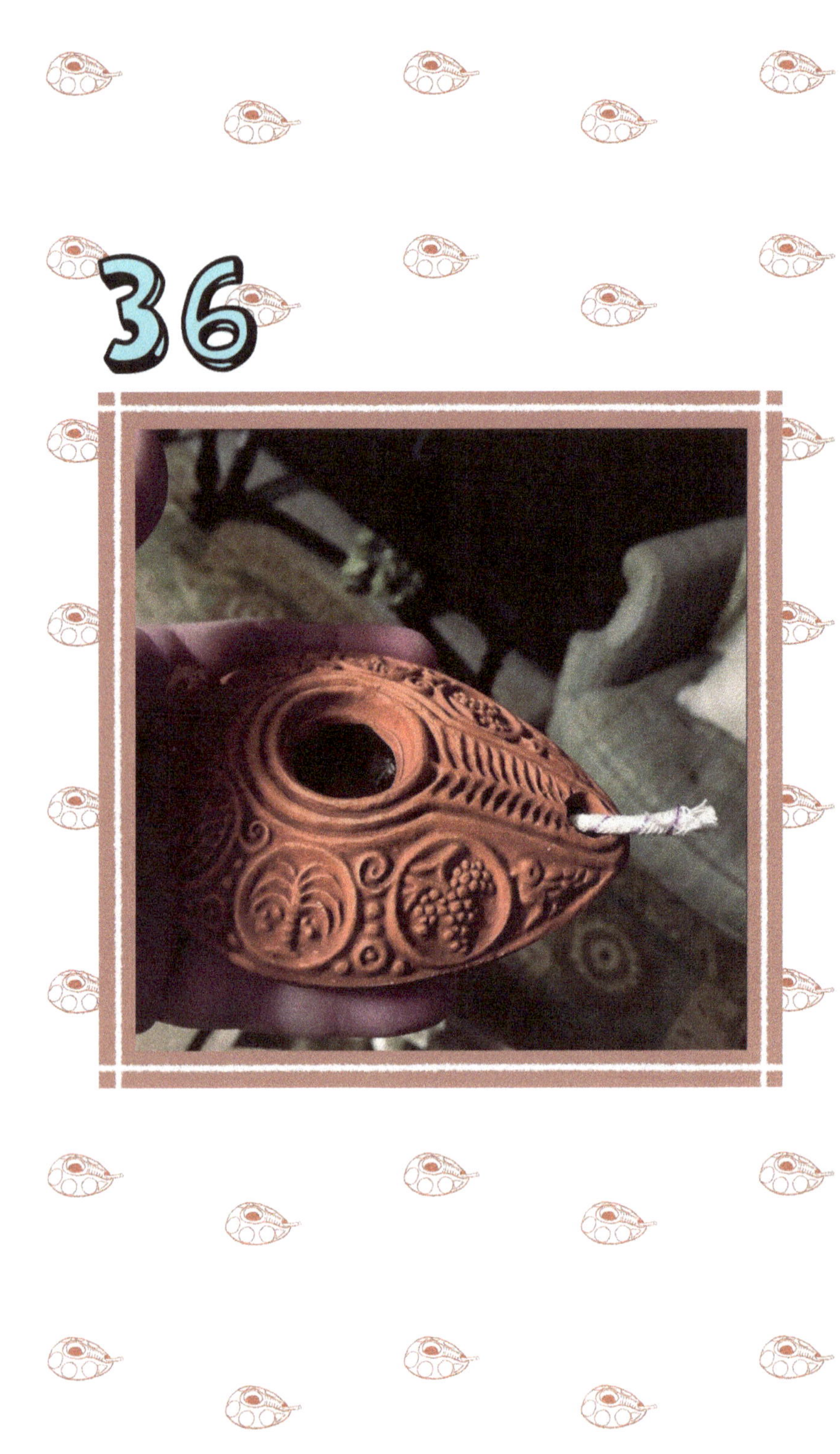

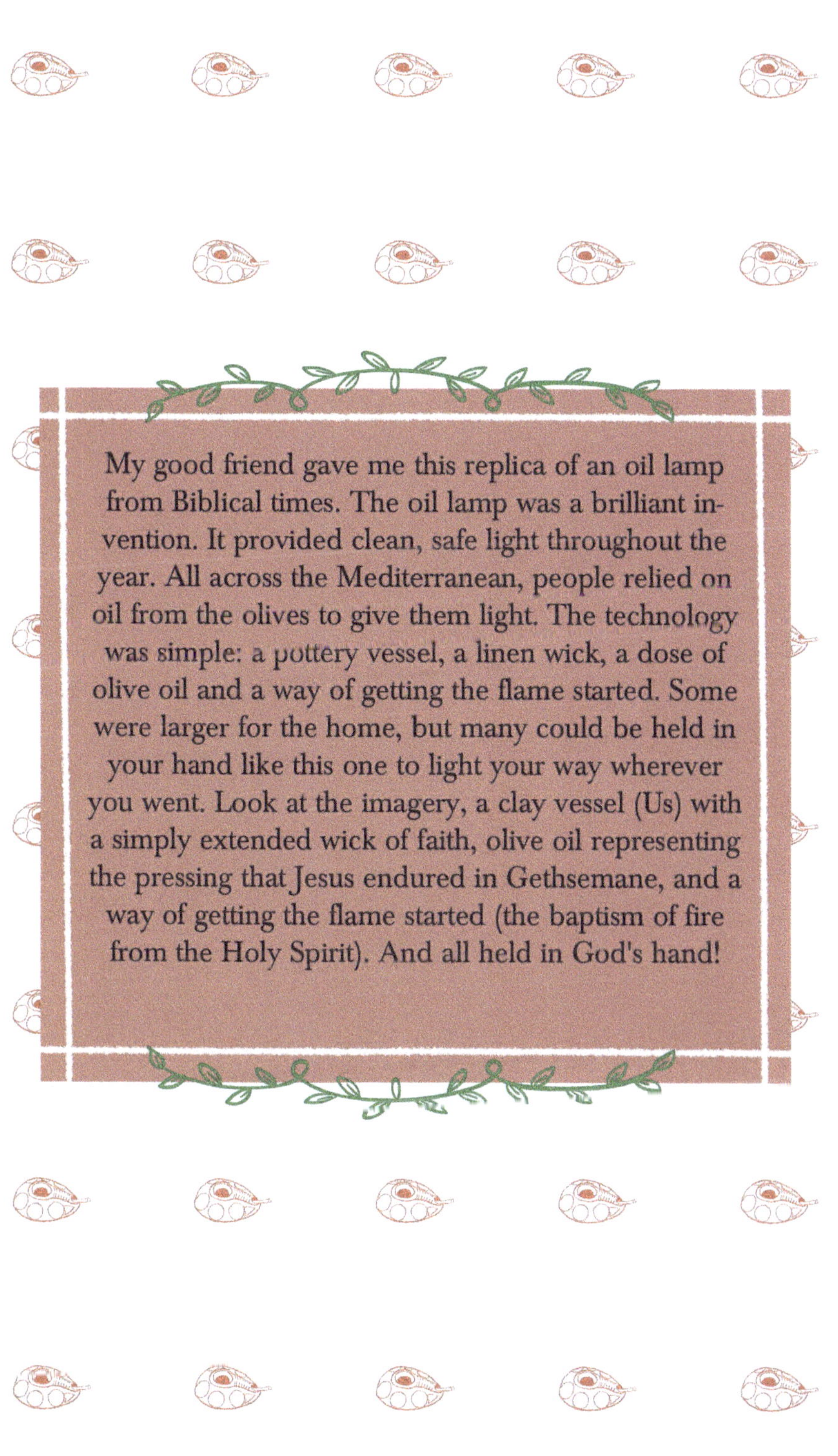

My good friend gave me this replica of an oil lamp from Biblical times. The oil lamp was a brilliant invention. It provided clean, safe light throughout the year. All across the Mediterranean, people relied on oil from the olives to give them light. The technology was simple: a pottery vessel, a linen wick, a dose of olive oil and a way of getting the flame started. Some were larger for the home, but many could be held in your hand like this one to light your way wherever you went. Look at the imagery, a clay vessel (Us) with a simply extended wick of faith, olive oil representing the pressing that Jesus endured in Gethsemane, and a way of getting the flame started (the baptism of fire from the Holy Spirit). And all held in God's hand!

37

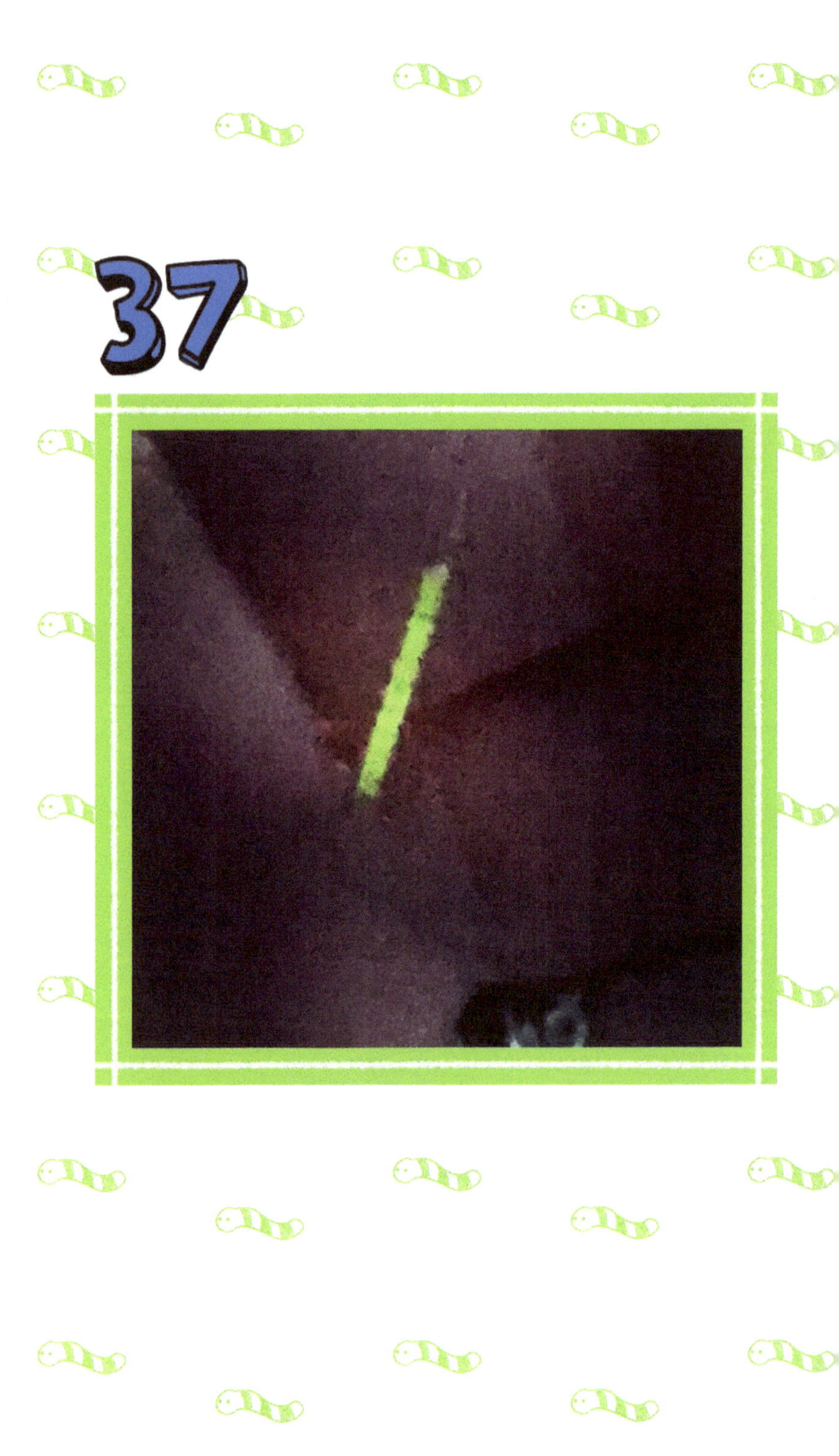

This tiny little inchworm was hanging midway between the leaf he came from and the ground beneath. He was so small that I had to put my hand behind him and zoom in to take his picture. I nearly missed him swinging on his invisible thread in the cool morning breeze. As he turned and hung there I thought how some days I feel like this little guy, just hanging there in the middle, having left where I was to make my way towards something new, something solid and sturdy and vast, something so much better for me than where I was. But as I make my way, I feel like I'm hanging by an invisible thread that still attaches me to my past, to my comfort, to my known experiences. I know deep in my heart that the place I am going is wide open and filled with endless possibilities. Still, until I reach it, I sometimes swing to the left or the right and consider scampering back to the place that I have come from even though I know it is in my nature, just like the inchworm, to travel the world and set my feet in new places! I am inspired by this brave little bug today. Although the force that holds him is invisible, it has been crafted to strongly sustain him as he goes.

38

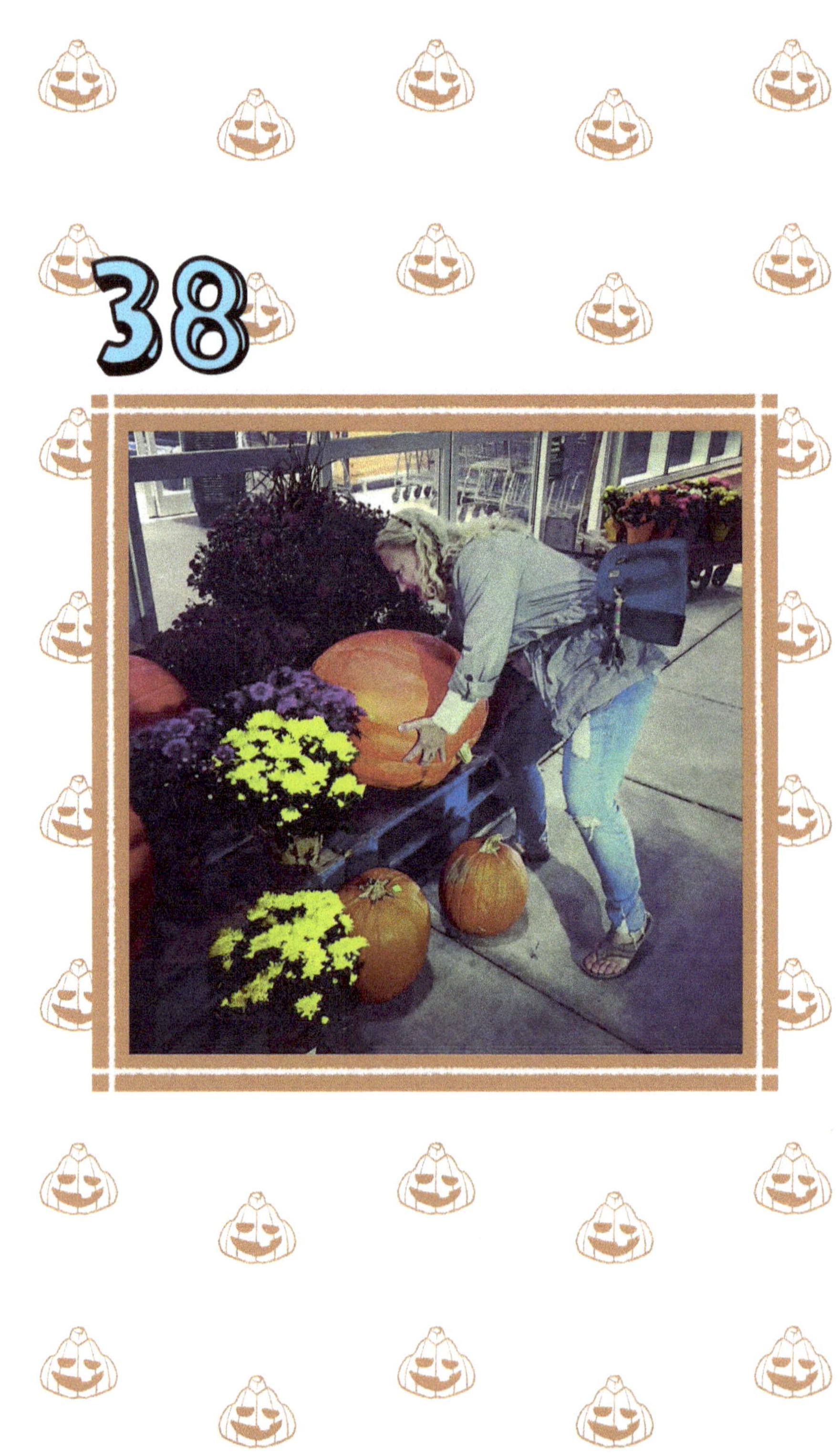

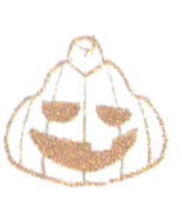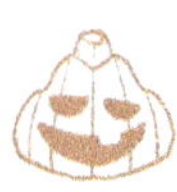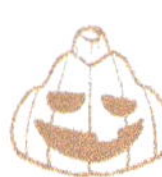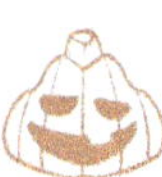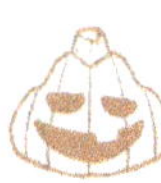
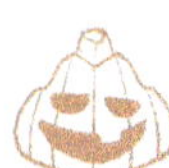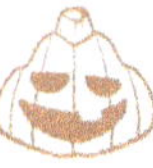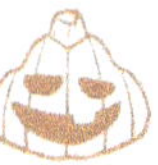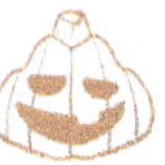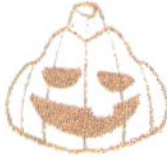

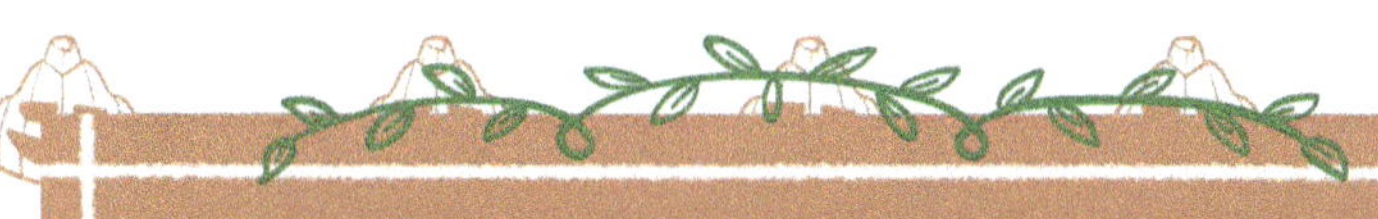

I was joking around asking, "How I will pick this up to put it in my cart? How will I go in and pay for it?"

When my friend took the picture of me joking around, it struck me that I often ask too many practical questions when God has something big planned for me to pick up. Instead of just marveling at the size and being grateful for the opportunity, I often ask how will it be done? If the one who created such a thing can make it, then why wouldn't He have a way for me to take it home? Some things are bigger than we can imagine. But nothing is too big for God!

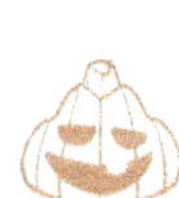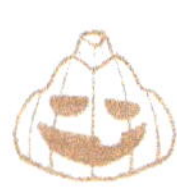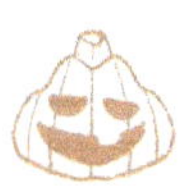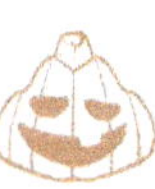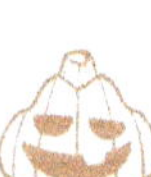
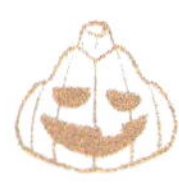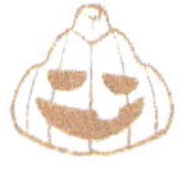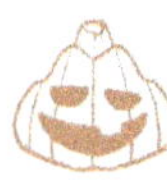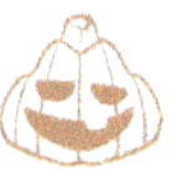

39

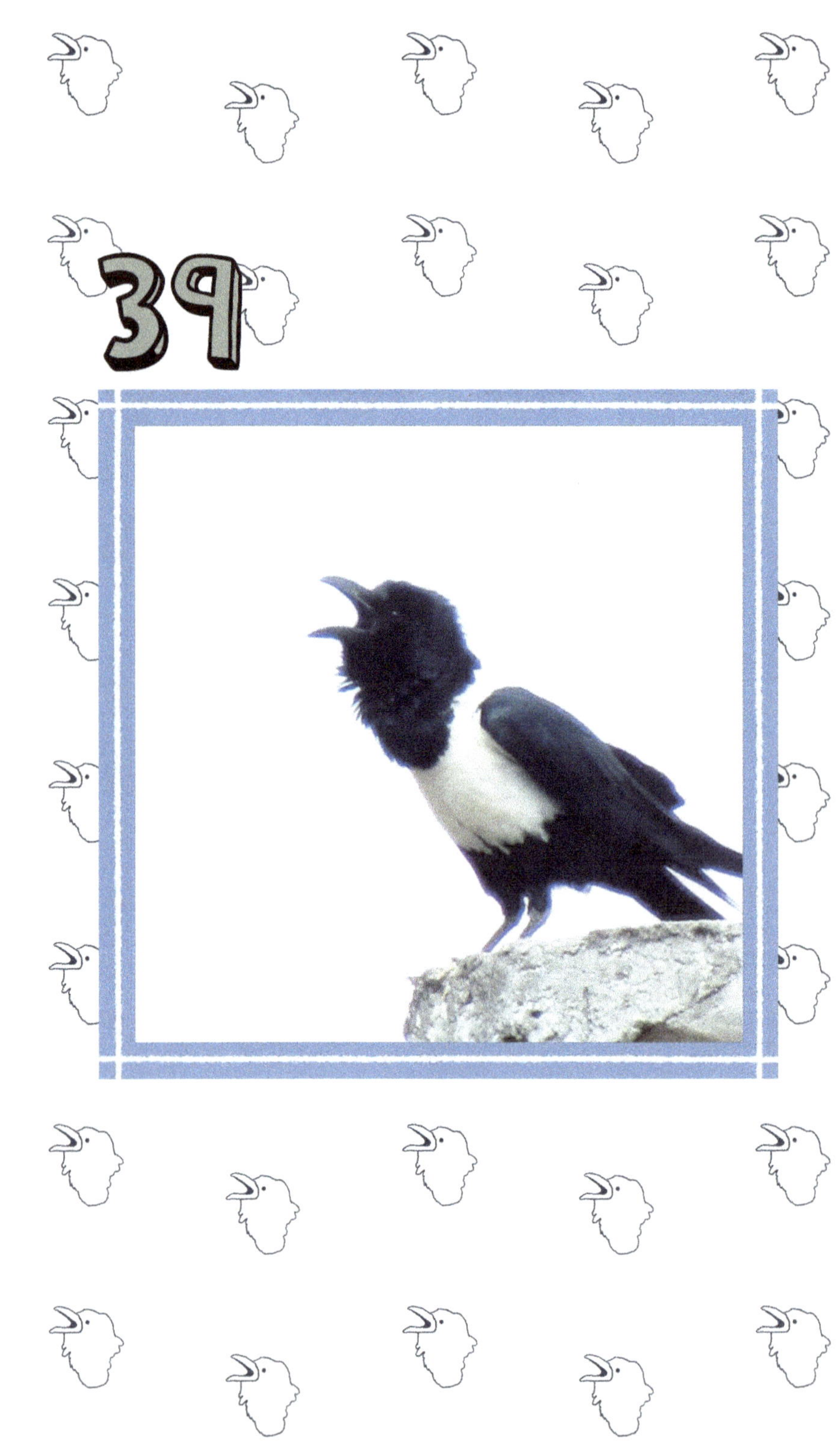

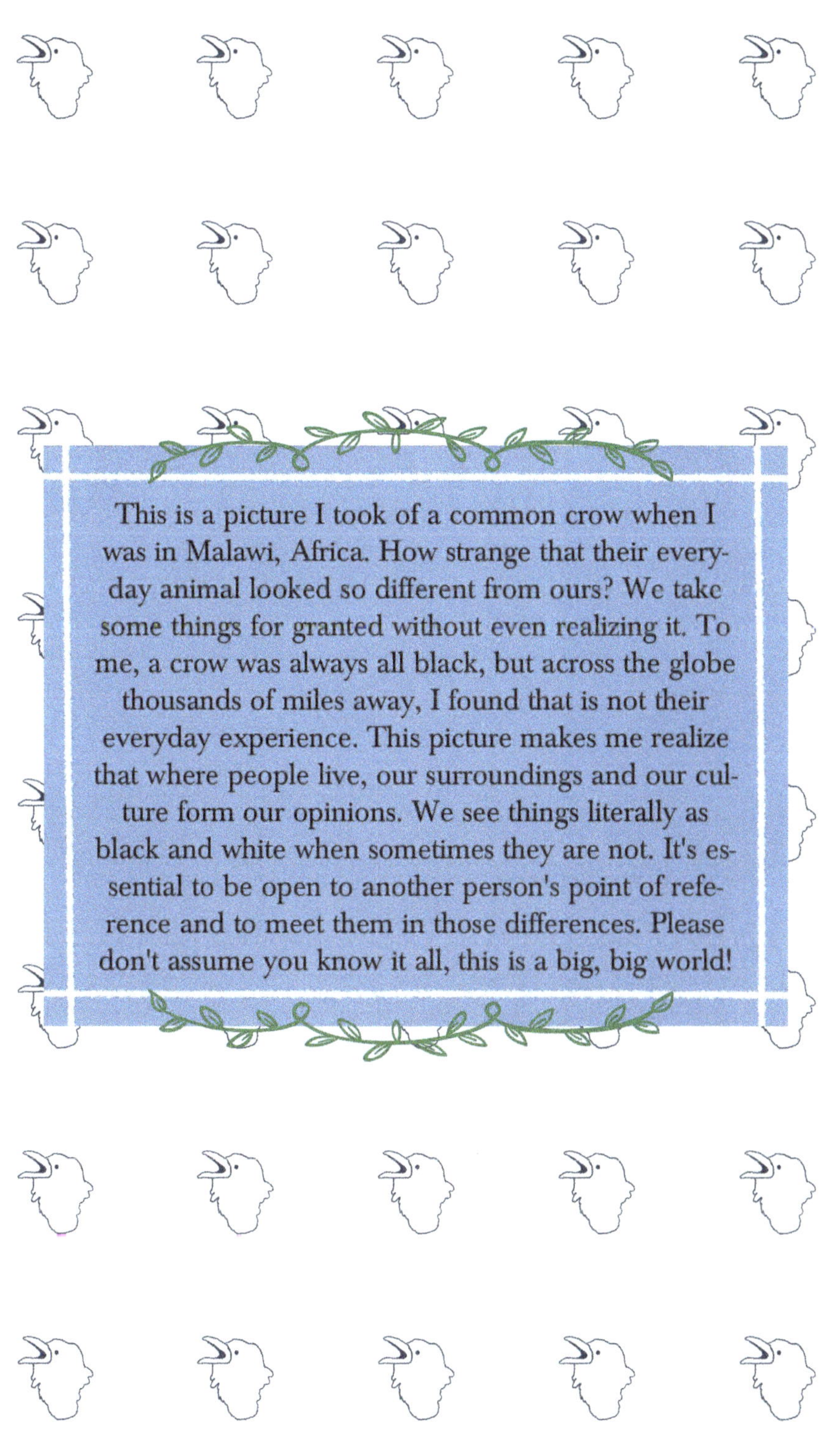

This is a picture I took of a common crow when I was in Malawi, Africa. How strange that their everyday animal looked so different from ours? We take some things for granted without even realizing it. To me, a crow was always all black, but across the globe thousands of miles away, I found that is not their everyday experience. This picture makes me realize that where people live, our surroundings and our culture form our opinions. We see things literally as black and white when sometimes they are not. It's essential to be open to another person's point of reference and to meet them in those differences. Please don't assume you know it all, this is a big, big world!

40

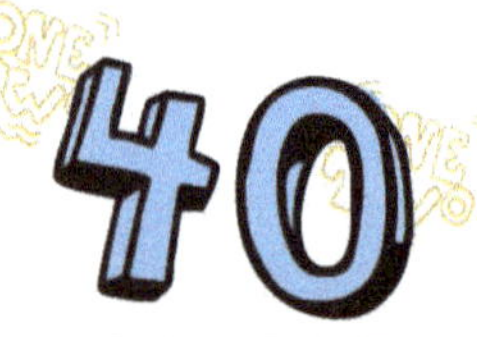

TWO
people are
better off
THAN
ONE
for they can help
each other
SUCCEED
ECC 4:9

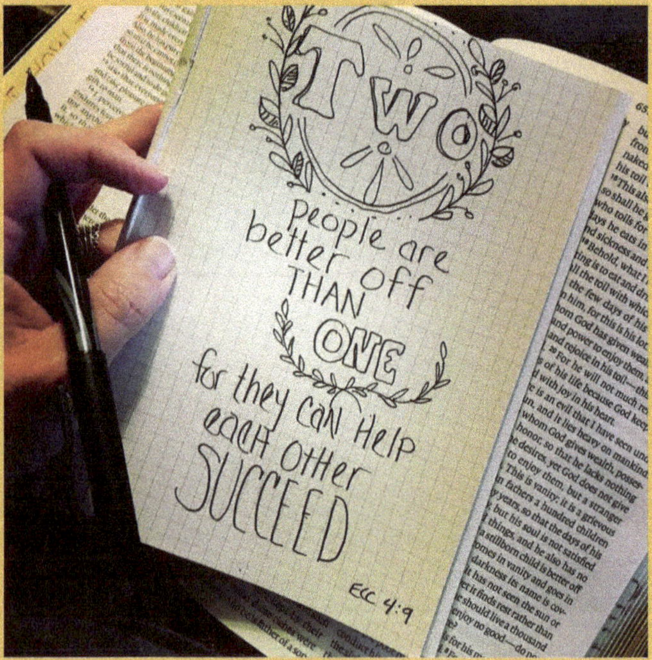

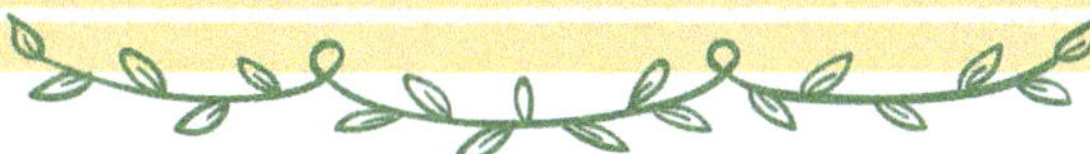

Stating that two are better than one is sound Biblical wisdom. We need each other. People can help each other. We can stand together; we can support one another in a society that says "Me first," and say, "How can I walk with you ?"